RUN WALK CRAWL

GETTING FIT IN MY FORTIES

TIM LEBBON

Published by Dreaming in Fire Press

PRAISE FOR 'RUN WALK CRAWL'

'The perfect mix of hilarity and inspiration! Tim's incredible story is an absolute must read for anyone who is questioning whether or not to take on some crazy challenge (spoiler: you'll never regret it!) as well as for those who are more long-in-the-tooth masochists. You'll struggle to find a story of personal transformation that is as belly laugh inducing and uplifting as this one!'

— CHRISSIE WELLINGTON, FOUR-TIME IRONMAN
WORLD CHAMPION

'Funny, engaging, and totally inspirational, I loved *Run Walk Crawl*. Even if you're a couch potato like me, it will have you contemplating heading out for a walk before tucking into a piece of cake. Because, as Tim Lebbon says, 'what's the point of it all without a pint and a piece of cake to celebrate with?' Filled with entertaining anecdotes, memories and race reports, *Run Walk Crawl* has something for exercise novices and experts alike. I *raced* through this book. Perfect pandemic reading.'

— SARAH PINBOROUGH, BESTSELLING AUTHOR OF
BEHIND HER EYES

'Brutally honest and wonderfully witty. Tim's story is inspiring and packed full of advice on how to turn your life around.'

'Apparently the body you have when you leave your forties is the one you keep. Luckily for Tim, he slayed his demons throughout his 5th decade and here he shares his thoughts, fears, tips, Jedi mind tricks and experiences in how he changed his life for the better. The perfect mix of humour and inspiration to bring out your inner weekend warrior, *Run Walk Crawl* is an essential read for anyone who is bored of their comfort zone.'

'Funny, witty, and full of useful advice. I wish I had read this book when I was starting my own journey into the world of endurance.'

AUTHOR'S NOTE

There's Ironman and there's an ironman. The former is the trademarked version of the latter. They're both long distance triathlons –– 2.4 mile swim, 112 mile bike ride, and finished off with a full marathon. For simplicity, I'll capitalise the word whenever I use it in this book. They're bloody hard, so it *needs* capitalising.

"No form of locomotion other than running, walking, or crawling is allowed."
— **Ironman UK race instructions (run section)**

INTRODUCTION

"Pain is inevitable. Suffering is optional."
— **Haruki Murakami**

I'm a professional horror writer with over forty novels, hundreds of short stories, half a dozen awards, and a couple of Hollywood movies to my name. You'd think that would prepare me for broken ribs, split nails, wetsuit burn that looks like Pedigree Chum ground down and mixed with tomato sauce, blisters the size of small household pets, cycling for three miles behind a guy wearing an all-white tri suit on a TT bike, and genital chafing.

You'd think. But nope.

Yes, I'm a horror writer, but I still have to sit down to stop myself from *falling* down if I cut my finger on a knife in the washing up bowl. I don't do blood. Especially my own. And reading and writing horror was in no way any preparation for some of the injuries, physical challenges, sights, and adventures I'd encounter when I decided, in my early forties, that it was time to get fit. I can write about supernatural terrors but still feel queasy when I see a runner pause, bend over, and hurl up a stew of energy bars, multi-coloured gels, and desperation. And a zombie apocalypse has got nothing on the last few miles of an Ironman run. It probably even smells better.

For those of you who like it quick—maybe you're more a fan of the short story than the novel, the espresso rather than the grande latte, or the sprint triathlon instead of the ironman—here's the short version:

On January 1st 2011, at the age of forty-one, I weighed close to fifteen stones (for my American friends that's 210 pounds). For a 5'8" chap this is scientifically known as 'pretty big'. It had been one of those Christmases I always promise myself won't happen—too much drink, too much food, borderline-illegal quantities of Quality Street, and nowhere near enough exercise. In fact around this time I wasn't exercising *at all*. A walk to the local shop for another bottle of wine was my idea of getting fit. On that New Year's Day we walked with a group of friends to a local pub up in the hills, a challenging, hilly 4 mile walk that I'd done many times before. It was harder than ever, and when we reached the splendid Goose & Cuckoo (my kids always called it the Gruesome Cuckoo, which appeals to my darker sensibilities) I was out of breath, heart thumping, and despite the chill in the air I was sweating like a sweaty thing.

I felt quite wretched—slothful, unfit, and it was getting so that I was disgusted with myself. Even finding something to wear on that walk had been a challenge, as I'd put on so much weight over that decadent Christmas season. I was in my 42nd year, and putting myself at risk of illness. I stood in the pub garden with my friends, contemplating the traditional bull-shit New Year's Resolution fitness regime that my wife Tracey and I always begin, and then end soon after— "No booze, healthier food ... " And I have a clear and distinct memory of looking at that 'one last pint' in my hand and not being able to see my own shoes to figure out whether my laces were undone or not, and thinking, *It's gone too far to turn around.* Weight gain, fitness loss, is insidious. It creeps. But that *it's gone too far* realisation was sudden, and it hit me hard. It was the first time I remember feeling my age. And it felt crap.

Six pints and a burger later we walked home. Downhill. And even that was a challenge.

Strangely, it wasn't that moment, that realisation, and that shunning of the 'fitness' resolution made just twelve hours earlier—at midnight on New Year's Eve, leaning against a wall clutching another whiskey and another sausage roll and seeing three Jools Hollands on the telly and wondering why the floor wasn't level anymore—that set the ball rolling towards me getting fit. If anything, that really was the moment I gave up. It sounds glib and self-indulgent, and I'm not throwing (as my daughter's good friend would say in her splendidly deep Welsh accent) "A fukkin pitttty paaarty!" But I really did think then that it was too late. I was forty-one years old. And I mean, *old!*

How the hell do you turn things around and get fit at that advanced age?

The changing point—the moment between my life before, and what my life is now, and yes that sounds painfully melodramatic, and yes my editor will probably tell me *this is a non-fiction book so try to be realistic, for fuck's sake!*—was bumping into a good friend I hadn't seen in a while. It was at a football or rugby training session for our kids, where the parents stood on the sidelines freezing off various body parts while the kids ran around like lunatics kicking the hell out of each other and coating themselves in as much mud as possible.

His name is Pete. Now, I'm sure Pete won't mind me saying that before, he'd always been a cheery, slightly chubby bloke. But when I saw him––slim, vigorous, healthy-looking––I did a double take. I asked what had happened. And his three-word response ignited something in me:

"I got fit."

Pivot point ... past life to future life ...

Pretty much that same day I committed to taking on the national Three Peaks Challenge along with Pete and three other friends. That involved climbing the three highest mountains in Scotland, England, and Wales (Ben Nevis, Scafell Pike, and Snowdon) all in the space of 24 hours, including travel time between them.

It was crazy. I could barely bend over to tie my own shoelaces (but hey I was 41, slip-ons were more than acceptable). But I'd always jokingly said that a challenge way beyond what I believed I might be capable of was what I needed to get fit. That challenge had now been presented, and accepted.

And now, to end this short version of the story, here's an even shorter version of the end that will end this short version:

I got fit. We conquered the Three Peaks. In 2012 I completed my first two marathons. I also bought a road bike, started learning how to swim, and took part in my first couple of triathlons. By 2013 I was 11st 8lbs (162 pounds) and had dropped from a 36" to a 30" waist. And in August of 2013 I completed my first Ironman race. It was one of the greatest days of my life, and getting there *changed* my life forever. For the rest of my forties I trained for, and competed in, a dozen half ironman races, four more iron distance events, half marathons and marathons, cycling events, and an ultra-marathon. I continued to enjoy a beer and more than just an occasional cake. And I'd found something that I loved so much that fitness almost became a by-product of this new way of life, not a final aim.

So that's what happened. A decade in two pages. But a lot more happened in that time, and it's led to a real change in my life and outlook. Triathlon and exercise has become a way of life, not just something I do to keep fit. As much a part of me as breathing and eating. I still like a beer. And it's *all* about the cake (in fact, I'll dedicate a whole chapter to cake. Because it's my book and I can, but I'm pretty sure if you've got the fitness bug and you've read this far, it's also certainly all about the cake for you, too. And the rubber and the lycra and creaming your gooch before a long bike ride, but that's for a different edition of *Run Walk Crawl* ...)

For those of you who like the slow burn of chafed thighs in an Ironman, or the more immersive experience of a longer take on things ... I present to you, The Rest of This Book. I'd like to stress, this is not an instruction manual or a training guide. Far from it, in fact, as I'll be quite up-front here and now in saying I'm pretty far from an elite athlete. I've never troubled a podium, I'm not *particularly* quick, and I often quip that if I ever qualify for Kona (the Ironman World Championships, qualification for which is run on an age-group basis) it'll be when I'm seventy-five. But I've also *never* not finished a race I've begun. I'm proud of that. And I've discovered a determination and levels of focus, fitness and endurance I'd have never, ever imagined I might have as I stood outside that pub on New Year's Day ten years ago and looked down through my half-empty pint, unable to see my feet past my expensively and expansively-wrought belly.

So this is simply a personal account of how getting fit in

my forties changed my life, and how exercise became a big part of my life. I'll talk about training and kit, mindset and physical challenges. I'll offer a few tips here and there, with the understanding that training is a very subjective endeavour. I'll talk about cake. Again. There'll be a few race reports, written back at the time I finished the races and tweaked only slightly to sit comfortably within these pages. I hope these race reports, as well as the rest of this short book, will communicate why I do this, why I love it so much, and just how exciting and painful and downright horrible and utterly bloody brilliant it can all sometimes be. And if it inspires you, and helps you catch the bug as well, I'd be delighted ... and I'll see you on the start line soon.

I've thought about writing this for a few years now, and sitting composing this introduction at the age of 51, I think I've had enough time to reflect on my past decade and realise, a) what the fuck was I thinking? and b) it's been the best ten years of my life. And those two polarised thoughts tend to book-end so many of the experiences I've had––the racing, the training, the buying of kit, the travelling, the 3am alarms just so that I can jump into a lake colder than a Polar bear's gonads with a thousand like-minded idiots:

"What the fuck am I doing?"

"I love this!"

If you've read this far––past the 'This is the short version' part of the introduction above––I'm guessing you're in the for the long haul. No special kit is required for reading this book, and you can have an energy gel-free hour or two. Just make sure you're sitting in a comfy chair and have a nice cup of coffee and a flapjack on the table next to you. And if some of you *are* wearing a sneaky pair of tri-shorts under your pyjama bottoms, or calf guards beneath your jeans, you're barking mad.

But I understand.

So, toes on the line. Heart rate elevated. Did you remember to anti-chafe cream your undercarriage?

Too late.

The gun fires, and we're on to Part One...

PART I

_____

FIRST STEPS

"Struggling and suffering are the essence of a life worth living. If you're not pushing yourself beyond the comfort zone, if you're not demanding more from yourself—expanding and learning as you go—you're choosing a numb existence. You're denying yourself an extraordinary trip." ─── **Dean Karnazes**

1

FINDING THE IMPOSSIBLE

So, the Three Peaks Challenge. Yeah, that'll be fun. Bit of walking, bit of climbing, plenty of time sat in the van in between, drinking coffee and eating. Sure. Loads of fun. And it can't be that hard. Can it?

21 miles of hiking ... 10,000 feet of climbing ... three mountains ... driving over 400 miles between climbs.

All in 24 hours.

We're gonna need a bigger cake.

The Three Peaks was without a doubt the most physically challenging event I'd ever considered undertaking. As I mentioned in the introduction, I'd always said to friends that in order to get myself fit, I'd have to sign up for something crazy. Something way beyond what I ever believed I'd be able to do. Something I thought was impossible. But for some reason I'd never done that, and never thought I would.

That's not to say I'd never tried getting fit. So to kick us off, here's a brief history of 'Fitness and Exercise in the Life of Tim'.

In school I was never any good at sports. Actually, strike that. I was never any good at *team* sports. With a choice of playing football or rugby during the winter I chose football, because it didn't appear to involve so much mud and violence. Of course, that proved untrue, because as one of those last-person-picked-to-be-on-the-team types I was invariably either put in goal or defence, positions as far away from the opposition's goal as possible, because anyone who had even an inkling about how to play only ever wanted to Score A Goal. The upshot of this was that, a) I never scored (not in the opposition team's goal, at least), and b) the violence I thought I'd avoided by not playing rugby was brought down upon be ten-fold by i) the other team's strikers as they kicked me out of the way in order to score, and ii) my own team's strikers when they kicked me for being kicked out of the way and letting the other team score.

Luckily by the time I hit the 4th year (I believe in modern times that's known as Year 10), us sad bastards who couldn't kick a ball were given the option of playing badminton indoors, which we grabbed onto with both hands. And that was fine. It was warmer indoors, the chance of severe injury was somewhat curtailed, and you didn't get covered in shit. Also, the PE teachers looked down on us a shirkers and less-than-human, so being unsupervised for ninety minutes meant we could sit and chat for an hour between ten-minute matches.

In the summer, we were given a similar option—play cricket, which as a sporting loser meant being put into bat last and being bowled out immediately, and then being cast out to the farthest point of the field and being mocked incessantly by the teacher if you failed to catch a ball struck by one of the Sporting Types that, given its hardness and trajectory, would likely cave in your skull unless you ran from its immediate path and hid behind the headmaster's car; or athletics.

The entire athletics programme at our school consisted of being told to fuck off to a field behind the main buildings and spend ninety minutes throwing spears at each other. The kill rate was relatively low, and I survived school without serious sporting injury.

During my school years I also joined Newport Canoe Club. I think my mum saw me as a bit of a loner (and someone in danger of being fat and unfit), and a friend of hers was a keen member. So she signed me up, and I loved it! I couldn't swim (not ideal for a watersport), but I countered that problem by doing my very best to never, ever actually make contact with the water. In canoe races this is a Good Thing, because capsizing inevitably meant that you didn't win. And surprisingly I *did* win quite a few races. I preferred the long distance river races (6 or 7 miles) to the sprints (500m or 1000m), because I was a nature lover, and racing along the rivers meant I had some birds to look at. Unfortunately (and please forgive the outdated terminology) as I passed my mid-teens the birds that interested me changed variety, and when training in Newport Docks and paddling amongst floating dead rats and oil slicks and turds, was balanced against trying to sneak into the local pubs for an illicit beer and completely failing to chat up some of the attractive girls there ... the training lost out. I drifted away from canoeing, which was a shame, because I was actually pretty good at it. My coach was a Hungarian chap called Frank, a lovely guy who'd won medals in the Commonwealth Games, and he thought I had the potential to do well.

In my late teens, having left school and started work as a surveyor with a local building firm, I joined a gym. I also started playing squash with a variety of friends, including a couple of girls I knew from school. I thought that a regular squash date would guarantee me some side benefits, but I completely failed to get off with either of them, and they always beat me.

In my twenties I carried on playing occasional games of squash, foregoing the additional stress of trying to get laid afterwards by getting married to my lovely wife Tracey, and usually playing squash with my mate Gareth, who I never fancied. I still lost, but we kept at it once a week, usually ending with a beer and a bag of crisps at the local, thereby undoing any slight benefit we'd gained by stumbling around the court and head-butting the glass screen.

I joined another gym.

In my thirties I bought a mountain bike and went for long, lonely rides in the countryside. Sometimes I did four, even five miles.

I joined another gym, this time with Tracey.

In my mid-thirties I started running. I look back on this period as my 'pre-getting fit in my forties' stage. 'Pre' because it wasn't my forties, but also because it didn't go exceedingly well. I did OK to start off with, increasing my running distance and actually signing up for a half marathon. I dropped some weight, got fitter and faster, and then on one eight mile run (four miles out, four miles back) I injured my knee at the turnaround and limped the four miles home.

I stopped running, let the knee heal, completely failed to start again, and joined another gym.

There's a pattern here. I didn't see it at the time. Or perhaps I did, but I didn't know what to do to change it. Through my teens, twenties and thirties, I exercised in a haphazard fashion with one distant aim in mind—to get fit. I joined gyms to get fit (sometimes I enjoyed going, especially when I joined with Tracey, but it would inevitably fade off...). I played squash, partly for fitness and partly for a bit of social interaction (any other more saucy interactions having not happened with the girls from school). All the exercise I did was to get fit.

It wasn't because I loved playing squash, or going to the gym, or back then even running. It was because I felt a pressure, maybe from society or from myself, but probably from both, to lose weight and be fit. And because I didn't love what I did, it inevitably fell by the wayside.

Fast forward to that day in January when I saw my mate Pete and asked what had happened to him and he said, "I got fit." And soon after, our commitment to do the Three Peaks. I now had an aim. Something tougher than anything I thought I'd ever be able to do. And that revealed something in me that I'd never known existed.

I like a challenge.

I'll talk about this more later. But back then, the concept of the Three Peaks excited me, even more so because I was so unfit and overweight that all I could imagine was my wretched corpse lying dead halfway up the first or second mountain (this actually almost happened on the third mountain ... but more of that soon). But because I was excited about it––I'm a real nature lover, and even now I'd rather a tough ten mile run in the local hills than ten miles on the road––I was driven to train so that I could complete it safely.

And because it was something I could barely even consider undertaking successfully, I took on the challenge and proceeded to kick it up the arse. I started reading the occasional book about fitness and training, eating better, and the five of us who were preparing to tackle the Three Peaks together started climbing the local hills.

And boy, did we climb.

I live close to the lovely market town of Abergavenny.

Surrounding the town are three hills—the Blorenge (whoever said that nothing rhymes with 'orange' can bite me), the Sugarloaf, and the Skirrid. Before starting to train for the Three Peaks I'd climbed all three of them with my wife and kids, and with friends, but I'd always viewed them as a bit of a challenge for a Sunday afternoon, followed by a drive home, a roast dinner the size of a table, and a grandad nap on the sofa (I now enjoy running up and down and around them all, but more of that later ... and that's a writery thing called foreshadowing).

We were incredibly lucky having these hills to train on. Each of them has its own distinct feel, from the short sharp shock of the Skirrid, to the tough frontal ascent of the Blorenge, to the longer winding routes up and around the Sugarloaf. We took them on in the day and night, anticipating a possible dark ascent of at least one of the mountains, and in doing so I discovered that...

...I really bloody enjoy this stuff!

For my first few walks I wore totally the wrong gear, and I can tell you that wearing a cotton tee shirt and sweating profusely as I hauled my almost-fifteen stone ass up a those steep slopes taught me an early lesson in the importance of appropriate kit. I bought walking boots, proper shorts, tech tee shirts that were designed to 'wick' moisture from your body (it sounded like magic. If it had worked, it would have been, but at least they dispersed sweat quickly and didn't mean you ended up feeling like you were carrying a ten-pound bag of washing around your waist). We got lost one misty morning descending the Sugarloaf, at which point my friend Russ told me an important tip—if you get lost coming down a hill, just go back to the top and start again. We trained all together, alone, and in pairs.

I quickly came to realise that I could do this stuff, and I

enjoyed it, but I needed to get fitter. So I started running. My mate Pete had been doing this for some time, but for me it had been a while. And even from the beginning there was something different about this. Last time I'd started running it had been to lose weight and get fit. This time it was so that I could do the Three Peaks Challenge. And I started to really enjoy it! My usual run went up gradually from two or three miles to five or six. I wasn't particularly fast, but I can still remember my first ever 'race'. It was a local fun run, a 5 mile loop out of the village and back again, and I loved every minute of it. I even passed the water station and, much to my wife's disgust, tipped a cup of water over my head. Yes, I was that person! But I didn't care, I was a runner now, and runners on the TV always did that, didn't they? I also beat some of the runners I was used to seeing training around the village. *Hold on,* I thought, *that's not supposed to happen!* I'm so non-competitive* that I even apologised to one of them for beating him.

*(I *thought* I wasn't competitive, but turned out I was, a little. I'll talk more about this later, too.)

We had several meetings to plan our trip (in the pub). We had use of a van big enough to comfortably carry us and our kit, we'd all have stints driving, and we bought every-thing we thought we'd need to be self-sustaining for a couple of days––dehydrated meals; chocolate bars; sports drinks; energy gels; water containers. We were without doubt over-prepared, but that's much better than the alternative.

Soon, the big weekend came. Were we ready? Had I trained enough? Would I die on Snowdon? (more clever foreshadowing ... and spoiler alert: no, I didn't. But I almost did). Would we complete the challenge in 24 hours?

It's like one of those James Bond films, isn't it, where he's in danger of being shot or cut in half by a lazer or eaten by an alligator, and you're on the edge of your seat because the scene is just so tense, even though if you really take a step back you know, *Of course he's going to escape. He's James fucking Bond!*

I'm not James Bond. But you already know I completed the challenge and went on to do lots of other stuff, otherwise this would be a pretty short book with a distinctly misleading title and you'd quite rightly ask for a refund.

But that's not to say it was at all easy, or went at all smoothly.

2

RACE REPORT:

THREE PEAKS CHALLENGE, JUNE 2011

Five men, one minibus, several hundred miles by road, 21 miles to walk, 10,000 feet to climb, 3 mountains to conquer, 24 hours to do it in, and fifteen pounds of jelly babies ... with stats like that, how could it not be epic?

We drove to Stirling on the Friday evening. That was a bloody long drive (for my American friends who are used to driving for 3 hours to have a coffee with someone, just give me a break ... it was almost 400 miles!) and stayed at Phil's cousin's house, a welcome change from our original plan— to arrive in Fort William at 2am and camp. After a few hours' sleep we headed for Fort William, stopping to fuel up on the way. (Note to roadside cafe: macaroni with onion and bacon usually tends to contain more than zero bits of bacon.) After that we killed an hour in Fort William, where I was forced to try on a huge tartan hat surrounded by unnatural amounts of fake ginger hair. I guess as the Bald One it was always going to be me, wasn't it? Much prompting could not persuade me to buy it and wear it up the mountain, out of fear of offending the locals.

Then we geared up for Ben Nevis. Arriving at the starting point, we realised just how many people would be climbing at the same time as us. They were like lines of multi-coloured ants snaking up the trail, zig-zagging across the mountain face until they became depressingly small and disappeared altogether. And they disappeared long before the summit.

This was one high bastard.

In good spirits, we set off. And though it is the highest of the three peaks by almost 1000 feet, I found this the easiest mountain to climb. The trails were steep, hard, and slippery (we all took at least one tumble). The smallish snow field was hard to climb, but fun to descend. The drifting mist soaked us and brought to mind Hammer horror films with cries in the distance, fleeting shadows, and the growls of creatures closing in ... but I was not hallucinating yet.

Everything I'd heard had told me that this would be the hardest of the three peaks. So when we reached the top, touched the trig point, took our photos, then hurried back down to arrive back at the van after four hours, 4400 feet, and 8 miles ... I was feeling pretty good about the whole thing.*

*(Of course, the fact that it was the first of the three, and we'd be climbing Snowdon exhausted and after having been awake for 24 hours or more, didn't cross my mind right then).

This was going to be a piece of cake! Talking of which, we all had a coffee and a piece of cake, as if to mock the Mountain Gods. Yeah, it was pretty easy until we stripped and changed by the roadside and were attacked by the infamous Scottish mozzies. But that's a horror story for another day.

First comedy mishap of the day occurred here (actually

this was the second. The first was Pete's headlong fall into a wet ditch three minutes after setting off, but I promised I wouldn't tell anyone about that, so I definitely won't). Tired and sweaty, I was preparing a recovery shake––one that came in powdered form which we had to mix with water–– when the bloody thing exploded all over me. I spent the rest of the day smelling of sickly-sweet reconstituted banana, however many times I changed or gave myself a wet-wiping (Perhaps this might account for my mixed relationship with bananas, more of which you can read about in my Ironman UK race report later).

It was 10pm by now, so we powered off into the night. We took it in turns driving south, icing our aching legs, massaging muscles to try and stop then seizing up. We were still buzzing from conquering Ben Nevis. It's not exactly the north face of the Eiger with Clint Eastwood on your tail, or free-climbing El Capitan, but for us it was the first third of *our* mountain for the day. And for me, I experienced a feeling I'd become more familiar with over the years and adventures to come––*I'm doing something amazing!*

This was beyond anything I'd ever done before, and I was so excited that I was actually doing an event I'd trained hard for. There were butterflies and a bit of nervousness, sure, but the excitement pretty much overshadowed that, and the sense of achievement––even before we'd finished, I know––was quite satisfying.

Yes, of course, there's a certain amount of ego involved in anything like this, and I'll also chat about that a bit more later. That, and competitiveness and personal betterment, are all tied up in the route I chose to take through my fifth decade on planet Earth, and they're a healthy part of getting fitter, pushing yourself more, challenging yourself, training, and achieving things you would have never considered possible.

There's also masochism. That's how many other people see it, anyway. The amount of people I've had telling me *You must be mad to do that* when I mention a race I've entered or a new challenging event I've zeroed in on, and in many ways I quite like that reaction. I *like* the idea that people think that some of the things I do are shifted several degrees from the norm. Maybe that's a bit more of that ego thing at enjoying the things I've achieved, but if it is, what the hell. I'll allow myself that.

So, back to our three peaks challenge, and there we were heading down the motorways of Scotland and northern England towards the Lake District. We were on a stopwatch here—remember, we had to climb three mountains and drive between them all within the 24 hour period—but it was still also really important to keep hydrated and fuelled up. Luckily among the five of us there were two, Russ and Phil, who had both done stuff like this before. Phil was very experienced in outdoor activities of many kinds, and a couple of months before our adventure he'd taken us on a map reading exercise on the beautiful hills around Llanthony Abbey. (*Huh*, I'd thought at the time, *why the hell will I need to read maps when we're walking up and down three of the most walked mountains in Britain?* Hmm. Hold that thought.) Russ was also very experienced at hill walking and had done some proper mountaineering, including tackling Mont Blanc solo. Proper mountaineering, I hoped, wouldn't be necessary here. So while me, Pete and Dave were keen to get the speed on, Russ and Phil made sure we kept our pace sensible. It's a good thing too, otherwise we'd have exhausted ourselves on the first mountain and that would have been that.

We stopped a couple of times on the way to the Lake District for food and toilet breaks, brewing up on a portable stove and eating rehydrated meals––honestly, not as bad as they sound; but I haven't eaten one since––and then we reached the twisting lanes of the beautiful Lake District and soon found ourselves ready to take on Scafell Pike.

It was very early morning when we set off. Phil had done this before, and he timed our efforts perfectly––a late afternoon start for Ben Nevis, long drive through the night to get to the base of Scafell Pike at 5 in the morning, leaving us plenty of time to get to Snowdon and tackle that mountain in the daylight as well. We had trained for nighttime walking, and we were tooled up with decent head torches, bivvy bags in case we got lost, and all the necessary safety equipment. But Phil ensured that our timings worked beautifully.

So, back to mountain number 2. Though our ascent was about 1200 feet less than Ben Nevis, I found this one really hard. The path was formed from random rocks, and was slippery and gritty. And steep. And once the paths ended and Scafell Pike's craggy summit came into view, the going changed to heavy boulders and scree fields, with no defined path to follow. With the numbers of people also completing the same challenge that day, it was also pretty difficult finding anywhere to take a pee! Honestly, though, by the time we were halfway up no one seemed particularly bothered by this, and I saw things I just can't erase from my mind. (Note: Nope. Still can't ten years later.)

It was a tough climb, and I'm sure if I ever return to Scafell Pike I'll like the place, but back then it wasn't a mountain I fell in love with. But we forged on, and after a last hard drag to the summit we touched the trig point, took our photos, then made like the sheep and got the flock out of there.

Ah yes, the weather! This is Britain after all, so you might wonder why I haven't been utterly preoccupied with how bloody terrible the weather was for our challenge. And the answer is: *Because it wasn't!* We were so, so lucky on Ben Nevis. The skies were cloudy, but we only ever experienced minor drizzle. At one point we were actually above the clouds, and when we walked down through them we'd obviously been above a major downpour, and that led to some nice slippery rocks and we saw a few people Bambi-ing their way down, but we remained dry. And on Scafell Pike, the weather was also pretty kind to us. It was bloody cold up there, and when you stop walking after a couple of hours and the wind hits your sweat-damped body ... that's chilling. But we'd trained for this and were prepared for the cold, both with our kit choices (like Shrek, we had layers), and mentally. Besides which, it was all part of the adventure.

Something I hadn't been prepared for was just how many people were doing the challenge at the same time. It makes sense, because we chose a weekend in June, when the daylight hours were longest, and that's when the mountains get really crowded with people doing the Three Peaks, either on their own or in larger organised events. But it still came as a bit of a shock ... this wasn't just 'us against the indifferent wilderness'. There were lines of people up and down the mountains, and sometimes we had to wait on steeper, more difficult ascents while those ahead of us moved on. As we climbed and descended Scafell Pike we were seeing lots of the same people we'd seen several hours and hundreds of miles away on Ben Nevis. Nods became 'hello's, and most people were good-natured and always ready with an encouraging comment. Apart from the big guy wearing a kid's teddy bear hat. 'Nice hat mate,' from me should have been met with a smile, at least. Miserable git.

Dress up looking like a dickhead, you've got to at least expect a few comments from passers by. Maybe he was suffering. Should have trained harder.

There was also a stag party doing the rounds, the stag wearing full walking gear along with a tutu and a blond wig. Hats off to him, he made Snowdon too, while at least half of his gang fell by the wayside.

We changed by the side of the road. Some people probably saw more than they would have liked, but I was tired and wet and didn't care and ... well, it had been cold up there. As we headed off along the beautiful winding lanes of the Lake District (I love that place and have been back several times since), the constant energy gels we'd been popping began to take effect on our stomachs, and Dave and I requested a pit-stop to let nature take its course.

And then, way out in the wild on top of a small hill by the side of the road, two portaloos! What the hell were they doing there? We didn't know, but Pete skidded to a stop and said, 'There you go.' And there, indeed, we went. And in a final stroke of fate, the doors didn't lock, and as we held them open we had a beautiful, panoramic view of Scafell Pike. I've never had such an essential sit-down in such a beautiful place.

What better way to thumb your nose at a mountain?

Time was ticking on. We had to get to Snowdon quickly, so we hit a roadside burger van and had a breakfast roll each to fuel up for the final climb. *Snowdon is the easiest,* I'd been told. *The paths are clear, and it's a gentle slog until the last hard climb. It'll be fine. Loads of people do it. Snowdon is the easiest...*

Bollocks.

Snowdon was a hell-hole. Or a hell-mountain. We'd been spoiled with the weather, and the following is a true story. Really. Doubt me, you doubters, but it's totally what happened.

I was driving. Dave was in the passenger seat beside me, while Pete, Russ and Phil were kipping in the mini-bus's back seats. We were listening to some great songs on the radio, and as we passed over the border from England into Wales, *Rain* by The Cult started playing. And rain started raining. Our luck with the weather had broken.

Luckily we found a place to park in the Pen-y-Pass car park (in retrospect, if that car park had been full that would probably have been our 24 hour attempt scuppered). We checked out the time, and realised that in order to reach the summit and get back down to the van and still meet the 24 hour target, we'd have to run as much as we could. Phil, ever-wise, had been assessing our fitness and preparedness throughout the day, and he suggested that Dave and Pete head off, leaving me, him and Russ to walk it. I disagreed, and said I should go with Dave and Pete. I'm glad I did ... but in many ways Phil was right, too. I was slowing down, getting tired, and with the weather the way it was, this mountain was going to be a bastard. It turned out to be the toughest thing I'd ever done.

So Dave, Pete and I jogged off, leaving Russ and Phil to take an easier pace. Into the rain. And as we started climbing, into the gale-force winds and driving mist as well.

We took the Miner's Track, which has a long winding approach to the mountain ending in a steep, tough climb right up to the summit. We started running, and already the puddles along the track were getting far too numerous to avoid, and in places they were up to our ankles. Pete, totally in the zone, pulled ahead of us. Dave and I ran and then climbed together, both developing painful knees that had us gritting our teeth against the discomfort. The weather was just horrible, with visibility down to maybe twenty metres. We were climbing waterfalls with numb hands. We stopped for an energy bar which neither of us could open with our frozen fingers. We were soaked from the outside with rain, and from the inside with sweat. But we were determined, and never once did either of us suggest that we wouldn't finish. Dave asked me to shoot him. I thought I probably wouldn't have the strength, or the feeling in my fingers, to pull the trigger.

There were still plenty of people climbing with us, and the route we took even in that weather seemed pretty clear to me. This assumption was a *big* mistake, which would return to bite me in the arse pretty soon.

This was getting gnarly, and the memory of our relatively easy ascents of the first two mountains was far in the past. I'd never done anything like this, ever, and mentally I found the going very tough. Dave and I urged each other on, and by the time we reached the top––my first time on Snowdon's summit, but far from the last––the wind was staggeringly strong, blowing rain into our faces that felt like shotgun pellets. My knee was knackered. I dragged myself the last couple of hundred feet and up those steps at the top of that horrible, beautiful mountain, only climbing with my left leg, and by the time I reached Dave at the trig point I was shivering with the pain. We shook hands ... we'd done it! In that awful weather, exhausted, wet, and cold, it was a sublime moment.

I honestly didn't shed a tear. It was the rain.

Dave decided to try and head down quickly to achieve the 24 hour time (Pete had already passed us on his descent). So he went, and I started down on my own. After a few hundred feet I met Russ and Phil on their way up, and I said I'd wait there for them and descend together. But Phil, ever wise to the ways of these mountains, told me I should move on alone, otherwise I'd risk freezing to death. The last thing I wanted was to be taken off the mountain by mountain rescue.

So I headed down on my own, and this was my rough time. I couldn't see, because my glasses were soaked and there was nothing dry to wipe them with (it was soon after this that I started wearing contacts for sport and exercise). But I kept a good speed, and for a while even thought I might make it down on time.

The string of climbers had thinned out by now, and somehow I overshot the path we'd taken on the way up that led down to the Miner's Track. If only I'd known I was now on the Pyg Track, which led eventually to the same place where we'd parked, I would have carried on. But I was tired, in pain, wet and extremely cold, suffering severely from sleep deprivation, and my knowledge of moving in the mountains really wasn't up to scratch. And this is when I made a mistake that could easily have resulted in me dying on Snowdon.

I knew by now that I'd overshot the path. *Dickhead*, I thought, but looking down when the high winds cleared the mist and clouds for a bit, I could see the lakes that the Miner's Track wound past. So I decided to leave the path and start heading down the mountainside towards the lower lakes.

Total dickhead, I think now.

I crawled and slid down the steep slope, and there was no one around me, and that should have sounded the alarm bells. A few minutes later I came to my senses a little––not sure how––realised what a stupid risky thing I was doing, and decided to backtrack. Russ's advice from one of our misty training walks came back to me: "If you get lost on the way down, go back to the top and start again." So I climbed back to the path, doubled back, and eventually found the route I should have taken back down to the Miner's Track.

By this time Russ and Phil had passed me and were making their way back to the van. I was past exhaustion, and I'd also passed the 24 hour limit. But I'd made the Snowdon summit within about 23 hours of starting at the base of Ben Nevis, so ... that was fine by me. I was starting to get worried that the other chaps would have all made it back and might be concerned I wasn't there. If Prince William had to pick me up with his chopper (something Kate is probably quite used to by now), I'd never live it down.

So after 10,000 feet of climbing, 32 hours with virtually no sleep, 18 miles walked, and the insane chaos of Snowdon, I somehow found the energy and strength to run the three miles back along the flatter portions of the Miner's Path. On the way, I looked up and found the slope I'd started descending an hour before. It ended in a hundred foot drop. I'm pretty sure that's the closest I've ever been to dying.

Back at Pen-y-Pass there was a cafe. It was warm. And dry. And I sat down with a very relieved Dave, Pete, Russ, and Phil—they'd been discussing calling mountain rescue to find my stupid ass—and drank a pint of very sweet tea. It was over. We ate a splendid meal at *Pete's Eats* in Llanberis (not the last time I'd eat here after a tough event), then somehow stayed awake to manage the drive home.

The Three Peaks Challenge has 'challenge' in the title for a reason. It was the hardest thing I had ever done, a true endurance event, but also one of the most enjoyable, and above all the most *satisfying*. It was always a challenge first and foremost for myself, but I also raised around £1,500 for a very worthy charity that's close to my heart.

Ten years later, looking back on those amazing couple of

days, I can say it was one of the most powerful learning experiences of my life. Everything started to change for me from the moment I chatted with Pete and committed to the Three Peaks, and over the next year or so that change was destined to continue.

I always say that Ironman changed my life, but training for and completing the Three Peaks was the moment that seeded the change. I'd taken on a challenge I honestly wasn't sure I could finish, and finished it.

In the van driving home I thought, *Never again*.

Next day, I was wondering what was next.

3

MORE

S ome people take on a big challenge, train for it, do it, and once it's achieved they've reached the top of their own personal mountain. They stop climbing. Once it's done, it's done, and what's the point in continuing? And if you don't enjoy this stuff—if you're training for a challenge just to do the challenge, and in doing so you don't develop a love for that training, that fitness, and that ability to do something you'd have thought impossible 6 months earlier—it's easy to fall back into those old ways.

I never worried that this would happen. Now, this is going to sound a bit wanky—I never intended this as a self-help book, or any sort of training guide, but an honest account of how I turned my fitness around in my almost-middle age, so here we go—in completing the Three Peaks I really surprised myself in several ways. And I'll talk about them now before getting into what came next ... and next ... and next:

First, the fitness levels I achieved in a relatively short time. I remember while we were training, Pete told me about the Forest of Dean 10k race, and my first reaction was,

Holy shit I could never run 10k! But I reconsidered, thought about how it would present a good mini-target on the way to the Three Peaks, and entered. I ran it in 53 minutes, which isn't super fast, but it's also not too shabby for a formerly overweight, edging-towards-middle-aged bloke. I'd shifted a couple of stones (over 30 pounds), and by the end of 2011 I could comfortably run a half marathon.

Second, just how much I loved this stuff! I'd fallen in love with running. I still liked *walking* in the local hills and mountains, but quickly found that I *loved* running in them. Trail running became my thing (and ten years later it still is). There's nothing better than heading out on a cool winter's morning, into the woods, splashing through mud and puddles, climbing a hillside up onto a local ridge, returning home ninety minutes later wet and cold, muddy and elated. I get scraped up by brambles, trip on stones, caught in rain showers, and I love it. Which might have something to do with the third discovery about myself that was the biggest surprise ...

... the mental side. I never knew that I possessed even a modicum of mental strength. In training for, and undertaking the races and challenges I talk about in this book, I've found a determination that frankly, and rather expletively, surprised the fuck of me. I honestly think that much of this comes from my first Ironman, which I'll talk about soon, but it surprised me because I'd never been particularly fit, and the idea of doing the Three Peaks, or running a marathon, or finishing an Ironman, had always seemed so ridiculous that they didn't even bear thinking about. Even now, after maybe 60 events, I've never started a race that I haven't finished. I know the time will come when that happens, but from somewhere I've manage to develop an 'I'm going to do this' attitude.

Perhaps, just perhaps, it's something that was seeded by my very favourite quote. Or maybe it's a proverb. Let's call it a quoverb. Anyway, I heard this when I started thinking about training for my first Ironman. It's about self belief, and if you can find that somewhere, somehow, some way, the sky really is the limit:

If you believe you can do something, or believe you can't, you're probably right.

So I'd finished the Three Peaks and I was wondering what was next. I loved running, and by the end of 2011 I was racing half marathons, including a couple of stunningly beautiful and tough coastal path races put on by the great organisation EnduranceLife.

But the big one was my target now—the marathon. Yet again it was one of those things I wasn't sure I could do. The step up from a half marathon to a full is a big one, and to continue this new lifestyle I'd discovered, I once again signed up for something that right then was probably beyond my abilities. I remember researching suitable marathons for the spring of 2012, looking for a race that was local-ish, not too big, and not city-based, because I much prefer running in the countryside. I didn't want to sign up for a trail marathon, because that would be madness! Just stupid! Crazy!*

*(I did one ten weeks after my first marathon).

So I settled on the North Dorset Village Marathon. A lovely scenic course, good reviews, smallish numbers (I think it was about 300 people running). I remember printing out the application and filling it out, and walking to the local post box at midnight to post my entry form and cheque. These were in those Dark, Distant Times before online entry, obviously. I walked back from posting the form on a high ... and woke up the next morning thinking, *Oh bloody hell I'm doing a marathon. Better start training.*

So I downloaded a training plan and started training.

I thoroughly recommend plans. They provide you with a structured approach, they're part of the learning process when you're training, and they build your training loads so that hopefully you don't end up getting injured. I talk a bit more about being coached later, but early on in my 40s fitness efforts I found generic training plans to be priceless. The marathon plan was sixteen weeks and the race was in May, so once the New Year rolled around—and *this* new year I *wasn't* rolling around, as I was over thirty pounds lighter than a year before—it began. There were three or four runs each week, with long runs at the weekend and structured, shorter runs during the week. I stuck to the plan when I could, and did my best to not agonise too much when I couldn't. I'm a writer and I work at home, but that doesn't mean I can just dump an afternoon's work to train, and at the time I also had two kids aged seven and twelve, so it was a careful balancing act between work, family, and training. Sometimes I found the balance, other times ... not quite.

Training for my first marathon was when I first encountered an interesting attitude from some people who I told about what I was doing. I've already mentioned how I quite like some reactions like, *You must be mad! I could never do that!* I often counter these claims, and I've told anyone who'll listen that a large proportion of the population could do an Ironman if they really, *really* wanted to, and they put their minds to it, and they did the training. But a lot of these comments come from people who don't really, *really* want to. Or even *really* want to. Or even want to. If someone laughs and tells me, *My exercise for the week is getting up from the sofa for another beer!* I'll smile and nod and let them get on with it. Each to their own, your mileage may vary, etc etc.

But sometimes the reactions are almost hostile, like the friend of a friend sitting on a sofa and telling me, *You're doing a marathon? You must be mad, people die doing that.* They're dead now. True story.

Soon after this race I would discover triathlon, which I'll talk a lot more about soon, and so since 2012 I've been training in three disciplines. But for this first marathon I just ran, and the more I trained the more optimistic my target time became. By the time the race was close I was planning on a sub-4 hour finish time. It was perfectly within my grasp, and I'd been running well with no injuries, following the training plan pretty well and getting the miles in.

There's an old military saying that says, *No plans survives first contact with the enemy.*

For my first marathon, my enemies were many and varied—inexperience; overconfidence; not sticking to the plan.

And cramp. Bloody hell ... the cramp!

4

RACE REPORT:

NORTH DORSET VILLAGE MARATHON, MAY 2012

A large part of endurance running is mental attitude. I've known that for a while. And I learned it for certain during my first marathon.

But that's not all I learned! During my first 26.2––the first half of which went very smoothly, the second half of which was a wretched, painful hell of leg cramps––I discovered a lot about myself and my running, good and bad.

The bad:

––I focussed too much on my time. After so long training so hard, I was too keen to finish in under 4 hours. I should have just run the race and enjoyed it. It was my first marathon, and to complete it would be an achievement in itself. But ... aiming for a 9 minute mile pace, for the first few miles I found myself hitting 8:40, sometimes 8:20. What I should have done was to pull back to 9:00, which is what my training had aimed at and how I'd visualised running the race. But adrenalin and excitement got the better of me. I was feeling good! Dickhead. Because at mile twelve, I started paying for that silly over-pacing when the muscle cramps of an epic scale began.

—I should have hydrated better. In truth I was very careful about this up until the morning of the race. I drank lots of water the days before, and all through the night (I kept waking in my B&B and taking a drink). I avoided alcohol for 2 weeks before the race. I ate well. But on the morning of the race, I probably didn't drink quite enough. My stupid reason? *I don't want to have to stop to piss all the way along the course.* Yeah, stupid stupid stupid. I didn't want to lose time. And at the first few water stops I took a swig or two and then threw the bottles. I should have walked and had a proper drink, or carried the bottles with me until they were finished. I didn't *feel* dehydrated. But when the cramps kicked in and didn't go ... well, they told their own story.

The good:

—My body is perfectly capable of running a marathon. I believed this before the race, and even though it was a struggle I still finished in 4:30. Post-race I was pretty pleased with how I did, and if I'd been kinder to my body (see above), it would have been a much more comfortable, faster run. I had no blisters at all, no chafing, I felt aerobically fit and capable. It was just those damn cramps.

—I have a strong mental attitude. And as I said above, this is the bit that surprised me the most! I love running, but I've always believed I don't push myself enough. But those last 14 miles of the marathon were ... quite horrible. I was in pain, struggling, but I was utterly determined to finish it. I'd trained so long and hard that to pull out (and there were two points when I truly thought I'd have to withdraw and appear on the results as a DNF), would have been a painful defeat. In the depths of the run, the idea of not finishing took on almost nightmarish proportions (I'd had a dream the night before that I didn't reach the start line in time!) How would I live with myself? How would I face everyone? But it was facing myself that made me finish. There was no other option, and crossing that line was one of the best, best moments.

There's more good than bad there. My finishing time wasn't terrible at all for a first try, I don't think, though the pain getting there was greater than it should have been.

AFTER THIS RACE I became a sucker for punishment. Ten weeks later I ran the Lakeland Trails Marathon, a complete circuit of Lake Coniston with another hilly boggy loop added on to get it up to marathon distance. I took a week off after my first marathon, and for the first couple of (very short) runs following that I had a pain in my knee. I felt shit. But of course there'd be pain after what I'd put myself through!

I learned a lot from that first race which made the Lakeland Trails marathon all the more enjoyable (I talk about this run a little more later). First, it's a run, not a race. I'm racing myself—I know I'll never win, I'm nowhere near fast enough. I set the pace at what I knew my body would be comfortable with, and didn't let the day's enthusiasms tells me otherwise. I also hydrated much better, and drank well all through the race, and yes, I did have to stop several times for a leak. But this was a trail race, and I was far from the only one! There were many startled sheep in those hills.

I finished my second marathon over an hour slower than my first (it was hilly, and tough, and muddy, and utterly beautiful and lovely), but I didn't once suffer cramps. My pacing, nutrition and hydration were much better, and I was pleased to learn those lessons.

They'd serve me well with what I had planned for 2013.

I'd already bought a bike and was interested in

triathlons. I couldn't swim even a length front crawl. So what? I'd never ridden a bike more than twenty miles. So what?

I entered a couple of sprint triathlons (relatively short distances), and the bug bit me, hard. I *loved* this! The triathlon community is inclusive and encouraging, and fuelled by excitement at finding a sport I loved so much—and by my desire to strive further and higher all the time—on September 10th I entered Ironman UK, set to take place almost a year later in 2013 in Bolton.

For those who don't know, an Ironman is an extreme triathlon involving a 2.4 mile swim, a 112 mile bike ride, and then a full marathon to finish. One person asked when I told them what I was doing, *How many days do you get to do that?*

The cut-off time is 17 hours.

I held the Ironman in terrified awe and read as much as I could about it, including personal accounts, training plans, advice books, magazine articles ... and horror stories. It was way, *way* beyond my capabilities, yet again, and right then it was pretty much beyond my comprehension. It was *terrifying.* And that was what made it so exciting.

Was I pushing myself one long, long step too far? As the Ironman saying goes, *Anything is Possible.*

5

ANYTHING IS POSSIBLE

My first ever triathlon was the City of Bath Triathlon, a sprint distance set in Bath University's superb sporting complex. The swim was in the excellent 50m pool, my first time in a pool that size, and I was the last swimmer in my wave to finish. With breast stroke. And I was cheered and clapped out of the pool like a bloody champ. That was my first experience of the support you get when you're racing a triathlon, and it's something that never gets old.

It was also my first time racing in a tri suit, and that took a bit of getting used to, because I've never been into bondage. A tri suit is designed to be worn across all three disciplines. So for the swim (if it's open water) you can wear a wetsuit over the top, and for the bike you can wear a cycling jersey over the top if it's chilly. It means no time-wasting changing in transition. And indeed, most transition areas––for shorter distances, at least––don't have changing tents, and nudity is usually banned. So, if you do decide to change between disciplines you'd have to struggle with a towel or changing robe. A tri suit makes all that unnecessary.

Although there was that time I saw a guy taking his wetsuit off to reveal he was naked underneath, and his foot got caught in one leg and he hopped around trying to get it out and the local birds were starting to take an interest ... yeah. Must've been a cold swim, that one.

For a first-timer like me, the tri suit felt like a second skin with a bit of padding on the butt for the bike leg. It leaves nothing to the imagination––there's nowhere to 'hide' anything, if you get my drift––and I spent some time in the changing room beforehand deciding which way I should 'dress'. Like my politics, I aimed to the left.

I loved every minute of this race. After the swim, it was a quick run in bare feet across bumpy ground to the bike. I got a bit of a telling off for mounting before the mount line, but in a friendly way, and I think my constant inane grin––*I'm racing my first triathlon!!!*––helped me on my way. The bike was hilly but fun, and I hit it hard and left nothing for the run. Two quick laps and I was a shaking wreck by the end, but I still crossed the line with a smile.

When the race was finished I remember wheeling my bike back to my car, proudly wearing my tee shirt (I still have it now) and thinking, *I'm a triathlete!* It was bloody brilliant.

This was before I'd signed up for Ironman UK, but the Ironman was already in my sights. My running was reasonable, and I already knew I could run a marathon. And I'd bought a bike just a couple of months before the City of Bath. In fact, I must have been my local bike shop's dream. I'd sold a bunch of expensive limited edition books from my collection for £800, and next day I walked into my local bike shop and said, *I need a helmet, some shoes, and a road bike.* I was like the Terminator, with cash and fewer muscles. They sold me a Giant Defy aluminium road bike, helmet, shoes, and a few other bits and pieces. I've still got that bike now, and though I haven't raced on it in years, I still love it. A great bit of kit. It was money very well spent, and it started a long relationship with my bike shop that would see me parting ways with a lot more cash in their premises.

So, with a couple of marathons under my belt, a bike in my office (the garage was too leaky and I didn't want my new treasure to get cold!), all I had to do was learn to swim. I could finish a sprint tri swimming breast stroke, but 2.4 miles in a lake was a different matter. At first I signed up for some coached group sessions at my local pool, but the coach seemed determined for some reason to get me swimming butterfly. Nope. Not necessary, thanks. I splashed around in the bottom lane, and I distinctly remember trying to swim a length front crawl and having to haul myself from the pool halfway along, out of breath and knackered. Hmmm, this wasn't going well.

I then did one of The Best Things I've Ever Done.*

*(After getting married and having kids, obviously. Just in case my wife and kids read this).

I joined a triathlon club.

I know I've stressed a few times that this isn't an instruction manual or a training book. It's not even an autobiography, really. Or maybe it's a bit of all three. But if I have one tip to offer anyone who's trying to get fit in their forties, it's this—join a club. Doesn't matter if it's a triathlon club, running club, kayaking or rugby or Zumba or pole dancing, whatever the hell sport you decide to have a go at after sitting on your arse through your twenties and thirties eating cake and getting bigger and more unfit, like I did.

Join a club!

My club is Newport and East Wales Triathlon (N.E.W.T). I've been a member now for almost 8 years, I've made so many friends there, and––Covid lockdown notwithstanding––I love training with them, whether it be intense swim sessions, social bike rides at the weekend (often with a coffee and cake stop of course), or hooking up with some members for a run now and then. I can only tell you about my experience, but I've found joining a club opened up so many horizons for me. It's inclusive and friendly, inspiring and supportive. There's a real mix of athletes there, from people who just go along for a training swim now and then, to semi-pro level triathletes and quali-fiers for Team GB or the Kona Triathlon World Champs. The coaches are amazing, well-qualified at what they do and, more importantly, passionate and eager to impart their knowledge. And it's like a great big family of people all with the same interests (triathlon and chocolate brownies).

And I almost didn't join. Why? Because I was nervous. Remember, I could hardly swim, and the joining require-ment was a 400m swim in under 12 minutes. I had my induction slot and I pulled out with a slight cold, twitchy about going and afraid that I'd not hit the time requirement (the coach at the time told me they're a training club, not a learn to swim club, and that's fair). So when I had a second date and plucked up the courage to go, I was delighted to swim my 400m in 9:59.

I was in! Straight into Lane 1, and from then on I swam once or twice each week, doing my best to improve, take on the tips and advice from coaches, and slowly but surely I got better. I can still remember being delighted when I was told to move up to Lane 2 ... a 43-year-old grinning as if I'd just been praised by my teacher! So I ducked under the rope, completely ignorant to the fact that each lane swims in opposite directions, and swam head-first into my friend Christine.

The benefits of being a club member are numerous, and it has absolutely helped me in so many ways––tips on training, kit, racing, races to enter, training plan advice, technique... and apart from all that, I've made lots of good friends. One of my favourite things to do is head out on Saturday on a group bike ride, no-one left behind. Even if you don't class yourself as a 'joiner' it'll be great for your training and racing. Or if you're like me you might get more involved with the club. I've been on the committee as social secretary, and now I help run our summer Aquathlon series.

I did a couple more shorter races, and in late 2012 I signed up for the Grafman half-Ironman the following year as a training race for Ironman UK. All my focus now was on the Ironman. It was still a ridiculous undertaking, beyond any concept of being achievable, but with encouragement from friends in the NEWTs, and family and friends outside the club, I began to believe that anything was possible.

That quote, again: *If you think you can do something, or think you can't, you're probably right.* Slowly, I went from *hoping* I could to *thinking* I could.

My swimming was coming along okay, and I was putting in miles on the bike. Long, cold, lonely, wet miles, through one of the worst winters in recent memory. That was a learning experience right there. Mainly, *wear more kit!*

Sometimes, I caught my wife looking at me strangely. We did have an occasional conversation about the level of training I was undertaking, and that's something that took me a bit of time to reconcile. I had this new, passionate pastime and an aim that was pushing me hard, both physically and mentally. But I also had a wife, young kids, and a job as a writer which meant if I didn't work, I didn't earn. It's said that training for an iron distance race is a selfish affair, and there's some truth in that, especially if you let yourself get completely drawn in. And Tracey wasn't used to this. She was used to a Tim who spent weekends at home, not a husband who got up on Saturday to bike for four hours in the rain and then ran ten or fifteen miles on the Sunday. It took a little while to find the right balance, and I made sure that I didn't put riding my bike ahead of watching my son play rugby or football, or turned down a social event in favour of a hard early-morning training session. It meant juggling days around, or sometimes missing sessions altogether, but as Tracey said to me several times—and as I've repeated to myself more than a few times over the years—*it's only a hobby.*

It is, true. But it's a hobby I'm passionate about, and over the years my training and racing have ceased to cause friction. I think for the first year or two, people might have viewed what I was doing as a fad or 'just a phase', but it's become a lot more than that. It's a way of life. And as I've said to Tracey on many occasions, *There are worst mid-life crises to have.**

*(I did buy a soft-top car in my late thirties, not quite mid-life (I hope!) but a fairly traditional crisis. Enjoying riding 100 miles in cold rain is much further down the list, although the rubber and lycra might confuse my hobby with other, more niche pastimes that many middle-agers take up.)

And it was interesting to gauge the reaction of other people around me, too, especially people who'd know me for a long time. My wife and kids saw me changing slowly over time, but I remember going to visit a relative and when she saw me she burst out crying, because she thought I was ill.

I should note here that during the latter stages of Ironman training, after months of massive bike rides, long swims, and runs constantly in the teens, it is common to have one's physical appearance compared to Yoda's ballsack.

And speaking of Yoda's ballsack, I should also mention here a couple of Andys who helped me through my Ironman training.

Andy Baxter was a first-time Ironman competitor like me, and the guy who started the Ironman Journey page on Facebook. A quick glance now tells me it currently has 40,000 members! Andy and I became online buddies, encouraging each other through training and only meeting for the first time at the Grafman, the half-distance race we'd entered as part of our training. I couldn't have done it without his constant encouragement and support.

Andy Holgate is well know in the Ironman community as the author of *Can't Swim, Can't Ride, Can't Run*, a book that has inspired countless people to take on the challenge. He was a big inspiration for me, too, and he became a sort of unofficial coach who I ended up contacting with problems and questions. Always helpful and friendly, under his Pirate nickname of IronHolgs he also features as a droid in an official *Star Wars* novel I wrote, *Into The Void*! Thank you, droid.

Now then, let's talk training plans again. For my first race a plan was essential, as I didn't really know what the hell I was doing. Luckily, someone at the club had already introduced me to Don Fink's brilliant book, *Be Iron-Fit*. This is a complete guide to Ironman training, including three training plans described as Finish It, Intermediate, and Competitive. Full of enthusiasm I went for the Competitive Plan, and I read it in detail from beginning to end. I became obsessed. Training *was* an obsession, because my focus on Ironman was so intense. I rarely had a week where I hit all the sessions, but I did my best, and tried not to be too anxious if I missed out a couple of days here and there. I was so focussed––and inexperienced––that I worried about not fitting in the correct swim session. I even asked the coach at swimming whether I could do the Fink sessions instead of the sessions set by the club. *Dickhead.* That's not what the coach said––she was very understanding, and put me at ease, saying that their sessions would get me to Ironman level just as well––but I'm pretty sure it's what she was thinking. And rightly so.

This was all new to me, and it felt great! I trained hard, fell off my bike, almost fell off a mountain, fell off my bike some more––I'd only been riding a road bike for four months, remember!––struggled with my swimming, and I felt a gradual but definite improvement in my fitness. My body shape changed, and though I'm sure I'll never look 'ripped', I looked better than I had in ... forever.

I picked up a knee injury late in my training which meant I didn't hit the heavy mileage on the bike and run, and in fact before the race I didn't cycle more than about 75 miles. That would come back to bite me, but I was so determined by now to finish the Ironman––the date was a point in my life beyond which I barely looked, and wouldn't have been able to see if I did––that I shut down the worry and just went with the flow.

Two years earlier I'd been forty pounds heavier and unfit, and the me of then wouldn't have recognised the me of now. I was about to undertake the toughest one-day endurance event on the planet. Sometimes, in darker moments running through the Sunday dawn, I didn't think I could do it. But I didn't want to think like that and be right.

6

RACE REPORT:

IRONMAN UK, BOLTON -- 4TH AUGUST, 2013

For the last 11 months I had trained, read everything I could about competing in Ironman, joined the NEWTs, taken whatever advice I could get ... and dreamed about crossing the finish line and hearing those thrilling words, *Tim, you are an Ironman!*

In truth, it had became something of an obsession. I'd got to know lots of other Ironman newbies, both in person and online, and I knew that I was not alone.

Now it was time.

On 2nd August I drove to Bolton with my family to try to make my Ironman dream come true.

Preparation

The journey up to Bolton was a bloody nightmare. Is it only in the UK where mile upon mile of traffic cones appear without any visible roadworks actually being undertaken? It was steaming hot, the car's air conditioning wasn't working, and what should have been a 3 hour journey stretched to more than 5 hours. I was getting more and more stressed, because I needed to get to Bolton town centre in time to register my kids Ellie and Dan for their Ironkids race, meet Andy Baxter (a fellow IM virgin), and get over to the out-of-town Reebok Stadium to register and attend the race briefing. As the slow motorway miles ticked by, I had less and less time. And getting more stressed is something I really didn't need ... already being nervous as hell about the race anyway!

Thankfully, we arrived just in time to register Dan and Ellie for Ironkids. After that we dropped our stuff off at the hotel, then we all took off to the Reebok Stadium. As the stress of the journey began to fade, this was when the pre-race nerves started to really jingle-jangle.

I'd never seen so many fit-looking people in one place. They all seemed to know what they were doing––laid back, confident, smiling, laughing. I felt intimidated and out of place. What was I doing here? Did I seriously think I could do this? But I gave myself a good talking to, and it was good having Tracey and the kids there with me, my race support team, supporting me already. Andy and I registered, received our Ironman wristbands (they always seem to trap a couple of arm hairs in there when they stick them on), collected our numbers and transition bags, then went to the race briefing.

Like a foot crushing a cartoon wannabe-triathlete in a Monty Python animation, a whole new level of nervousness settled down on me. The briefing was an upbeat talk, inspirational, but also businesslike, with lots of emphasis on what *not* to do (don't litter, draft, run down the finishing chute with a loved one ... or else you'll be disqualified). But when the guy asked how many were first-timers, and about

50% of those in the hall put up their hands, I started to feel a little better.

After the briefing, Andy B and his family headed back to the hotel and we hit Frankie and Benny's for a spot of dinner. There were Ironman wristbands all over the place, and I exchanged a few nervous smiles with fellow competitors. Lots of pasta and pizza was being eaten. Carb loading was the order of the day.

I was getting excited, but still nervous, and very conscious of how my knee was feeling.

A strained knee ligament is the injury that had kept me from proper training for the 6 or 7 weeks leading up to Ironman. I'd done plenty of swimming, but not much biking, and no running. I'd been following the Fink competitive training plan, and as the most intensive training period is in the final eight weeks before the race, I'd missed out on most of my long rides and runs. The longest ride I did before Ironman was 73 miles, the longest run 14 miles. Not the best prep for the biggest, longest, hardest race of my life.

Hence the nerves. And the feeling that my stomach was filled with small, clawed, toothed mammals all turning and running around and trying to bite each other, but missing and actually biting me.

We returned to the hotel and had a quick drink in the bar with Andy and his family. I had one pint, thinking it'd help me sleep. Then I spent an hour alone in my room preparing my kit and transition bags. Each bag had to have exactly what I needed in it. There was the T1 bag (swim to bike transition, with bike shoes, helmet, food, and all essential bike tools and kit); T2 (bike to run ... running shoes and socks, change of contact lenses, other bits and pieces); and the dry bag, containing the clothes I'd travel to the start in the following day, and everything I'd need at the finish.

I only checked the bags three times, because of course after the first and second times the Race Gremlins would invade my room and take out my bike shoes and leave them in the wardrobe or something, so I'd have to check again that they were in the correct bag, and what if my number belt had gone missing with my race number, even though I'd only seen it in there five minutes earlier?

You know the drill. Or if you don't, you will.

Eventually, after checking my bags a couple more times and ticking off items on my list (Tip: always make a kit list!) *again,* I turned in for an early night.

On Saturday morning it was time for Ironkids! It was a real thrill watching my daughter Ellie and son Dan racing down the Ironman UK finishers' red carpet, and they loved it too, putting in great performances. I was also delighted to meet a guy who'd become a good friend without us actually meeting ... Andy Holgate.

Andy is a 5-time Ironman finisher, and is probably one of the main reasons I started to believe that finishing an Ironman was possible. His book *Can't Swim, Can't Ride, Can't Run* is incredibly inspirational, charting his own journey from unfit overweight bloke to Ironman athlete. We'd become online friends––one of the weirder aspects of the 21st Century, and yet so true––and he had become something of a mentor and coach. I'd bombarded him with questions, and he was always ready with a reasoned, sensible reply. Beyond anything, he was always immensely encouraging, and it was obvious that he loved inspiring other people to do what he had done.

He spotted me before the Ironkids races and we chatted, drank coffee, and watched the races. Andy Baxter and I picked his brain for any last minute advice. He's a generous guy, so passionate about the sport, and like a droid in a *Star*

Wars novel (check out the name Ironholgs on Wookiepedia), he'll appear again later in this story.

The race had split transitions, with the start and Transition 1 (T1), Transition 2 (T2), and the finish all in different places. So once Ironkids was done, Andy B and I headed out to drop off our bike and bags at T1 and drive the bike course. We took my son Dan along—I told him it was that, or go shopping with my wife and daughter!

More nerves tingled upon arriving at Pennington Flash (location of the race start), seeing the choppy waters of the lake, the hundreds of bikes racked, the other transition bags already hanging there, and knowing that within a little over 12 hours the race would be underway. My Giant was probably the cheapest there, and it was the first time I'd seen what £2,000,000 worth of bikes looked like in one place. I comforted myself with the thought, *It's not the bike, it's the engine that drives it.* I'd have cause to remember that again the following day.

My knee felt ... OK. Was I confident? Quietly.

We drove the bike course. Though it's 112 miles, the bulk of it is covered in three large laps, so we only had to drive about 40 miles. It didn't seem too bad, and the one bad hill everyone had been talking about, Sheep House Lane, was a bit tasty, but no worse than many I ride where I live. *I've done the Blaenafon Triathlon*, I kept thinking as we drove up, and up (more about that tough race later). And there was a reward. The view from the top was beautiful, and the long, sweeping descents would be loads of fun, and free speed. After a long uphill drag, there's nothing like a swift descent to nudge up your average speed.

That evening my family and I hit Pizza Hut. *Lots* of nerves now. And there were lots of Ironman wristbands on view here, as well. My appetite was not huge, but I forced some food down. Pizza ... the supper of champions.

Because we'd paid for two hotel rooms, I had one to myself that night. So I bid my family an emotional good-night. Tracey gave me a hug and some whispered words of encouragement, "Just fucking do it." My kids did the same, with less swearing. I was welling up. It really struck me then just how much this was about my family, not just me. I'd lived Ironman for half a year, training hard, talking about it, worrying, daydreaming ... and in a very real way, so had Tracey, Ellie, and Dan.

And it had all come down to this. The next time I saw my wife and kids would hopefully be on the first lap of the marathon into Bolton. We'd arranged where they'd be spectating. I left the room, and I was on my own.

I slept reasonably well, considering, and after about 4 hours the alarm woke me at 2:30am for breakfast. I ate some bloody vile instant porridge, a banana, toast and jam, couple of cups of tea. Then Andy B drove us through a busy Bolton town centre to Reebok Stadium. Bolton was still filled with drunks at 4am, and the contrast struck me as surreal. They were puking and staggering and sleeping in gutters, while we were off to undertake the hardest one-day endurance event in the world!

From the Reebok Stadium we jumped on the shuttle bus to Pennington Flash, surrounded by fellow athletes. Strange word, that, and one that I'd never thought I could use to label myself. But things change, and I'd trained hard for this.

We didn't chat much. No one on the bus did. I think the sheer size of what I'd taken on was really hitting home, and I felt a bit sick. But I was also excited about what was to come. I'd trained for close on a year with this one single day in mind, and whatever might happen––knee giving way, exhaustion, bike crash, punctures, cramp—I was going to do my bloody best.

I was also racing in my dear Mum's memory. She'd died several years before from breast cancer, and she was at the forefront of my mind as I mentally prepared myself. I knew that she'd be proud of how far I'd come, and today I was determined to make her prouder still. I was also raising money for St David's Hospice Care, the organisation that did so much to look after her at home before she died.

"Just be bloody careful!" she'd have said. I resolved to do my best.

Swim

Bike uncovered, food stored in bike bag, tyre pressures checked, last visit to the loo, wetsuit on, dry bag dumped ... and it was amazing how time was galloping on towards the start.

The ten minutes before the swim was the worst nerves-wise. I stood with Andy B in the crowd of 1,600 athletes waiting to enter the water, and again we weren't chatting much. I think all the talking was going on inside our heads. We shook hands, wished each other good luck, and entered the water.

I was keen not to start too close to the front, as the deep-water start was one of the things worrying me most. I'd heard stories about how violent a mass-start could be—people being swum over, punched, kicked, wetsuits ripped, panic setting in...

The klaxon fired, I started my watch, and all my nerves instantly vanished. In their place was an intense, almost hysterical excitement—(*This was it, a year of preparation, training, worry and confidence building, and now I was racing an*

Ironman!)--and I couldn't help smiling. As it turned out I had started closer to the front than the back, but the washing machine must have been on slow spin. I received and gave a few accidental punches and kicks, but nothing too bad, and I soon settle into a rhythm.

It was a two lap course, and the first turn buoy must have been 800m away. It wasn't easy to sight. And it was my sighting that caused me most problems on the swim, especially on the return leg when we were swimming into the rising sun. If I'd been in the lake alone it would have been fine, but with hundreds of other people around me, splashing water and slashing arms threw up spray that the low sun seemed to catch on fire, dazzling me and confusing my sense of direction. My swimming felt good and steady, but I was worried about just where the hell I was going. I did what I knew you should never do in a race like this-- followed the person in front.

Turns out they must have been swimming in roughly the right direction. With lap one done in about 42 minutes (and I was very pleased with that), I started lap 2 confident and calmer than before. This second lap was pretty uneventful, other than a few more collisions. I again made the mistake of following other swimmers as they also zig-zagged into the sunrise, and instead of 2.4 I reckon I probably swam more like 2.7 miles. I also managed to pee in my wetsuit for the first time ever, in an effort to save time in transition. Achievement unlocked! Must admit I had to pause and bob a bit to do so.

Out of the water in 1:31, wetsuit stripped to my waist, the support at the swim exit was amazing. Hundreds of people lined the route into T1, shouting and cheering everyone along. It felt fantastic. All nerves had vanished, the swim was done, and now I was just out to enjoy the day.

Somehow I spent 7 minutes in T1, but the time went quickly. I grabbed my bike and hobbled on bike shoes out to the mount line, and the first part of my race was done.

Bike

Within a couple of hundred metres I knew something was wrong with my bike computer (moral of this story ... don't rely on tech!). I'd replaced the batteries, and in doing so it had reset to km/h. I didn't know how to switch it to mph, and with my contact lenses in it was difficult looking at things up close. So I left it, and spent the next couple of miles trying to mentally convert what km/h speed I'd have to hit to stick to my intended target pace of 17mph.

The 112 mile bike stage involved a point to point ride of about 14 miles, then three laps of about 33 miles. It was a nice ride on mostly closed roads. Even roads that weren't closed were heavily controlled, with cyclists being given right of way. Excellently organised and planned, it made for a (mostly) safe and enjoyable ride. There was one incident I saw on an open road where one wanker in a souped-up, crappy car screamed along the road beside cyclists, and when a car came in the opposite direction he had to slam on the anchors. He came so close to a collision, and he'd have taken out at least three cyclists if that had happened. He left with abuse ringing in his ears from plenty of people, but I suspect he hears that a lot.

Once I started the first of the three laps, the support really amped up. I heard the famous Colt Alley before I saw it (COLT—City of Lancaster Triathlon), and then a guy leaned into the road when he saw me and screamed in what was without doubt the loudest voice I heard that day, "COME ON TIM!" It was Andy Holgate, and the sheer

enthusiasm and delight he and his fellow Colt supporters
exuded powered me up the next hill.

I was delighted to hear another "Go, Tim!" from Hannah
and Rich, coaches from NEWT. I didn't know they'd be
there and it was a really nice boost.

I quickly came to the infamous, feared Sheep House
Lane. There must have been five hundred people on the
green at the bottom of the hill, waving banners, cheering,
offering shouts of encouragement to people they'd come to
support and everyone else as well. One sign read, *Toenails
are overrated*. Another, held by a little girl, said simply, *You're
all heroes*. It was quite overwhelming, and it wasn't the last
time that day that I'd find myself welling up. The intense
physical exertion undoubtedly does something to your
emotions. But it was also the fact that I kept thinking, *This is
it!* This place was the point where I'd be turning off to head
for T2 in a few hours' time, but for now there was the bulk
of the bike course still ahead of me.

I didn't find the hill too bad, and I overtook plenty of
people going up. That's a big advantage of living in Wales,
where there are severe inclines within a mile of my house in
any direction. The support was massive going up the hill,
people choosing places were racers would be going slow
enough to see properly. There was plenty of writing chalked
on the road, too, including the delightful *Sweating Like A Pig*.
Obviously aimed at someone in particular, but right then it
fit pretty much everyone.

At the top of the hill on the moorland was a camper van,
music blasting, and a load of guys in mankinis and wacky
wigs. Cheering, shouting, prancing, posing, having a drink,
they were fantastic, and later I was surprised to see them
there for laps two and three. They must have been freezing!
And probably almost as chafed as the competitors.

What goes up must come down, and after hitting the top of the hill and enjoying some glorious views, the big sweeping descents began. They seemed to go on forever and I reached over 40mph several times. Great fun, and a nice way to see the average speed knocked upwards after the hill climbs.

The next few miles of the course were a bit more lonely, with support in a few random places. I was eating regularly on the bike, trying to replace some of the ten thousand calories an average athlete burns during an Ironman. Many people had told me, *It's all about the bike.* Finish the bike fit to run, and you'll finish the race. And staying hydrated and fuelled was vital.

One of the great aspects of the race is having your name on your number. It worked on the bike and was even better on the run, and that small personal touch really gave me a boost at times. Kids loved it especially, shouting "Go on Tim!" when I passed. I did lots of waving over my shoulder.

My average speed was hanging around the 27 km/h mark, I was still eating and drinking well (I hate Powerbars. There, I've said it. They taste like cattle feed, and if I hadn't also taken along some of my homemade flapjacks, I think I might have puked). I also picked up plenty of bananas at the feed stations, and here's where I started to hate bananas because of a stupid mistake––I peeled the halved bananas with my teeth, and banana skin taste horrible! It was only after the race, back training with the club, when someone said, "Why didn't you just squeeze the banana out of its skin?"

Numpty.

The second lap went well. I saw a few competitors taking a rest by the roadside, one guy had taken a tumble and was being helped up, a few more with mechanical issues. I cruised on, taking care to eat and drink well—I must have eaten 4 bananas on the bike course. Another jet-engine volume "COME ON TIM!" from Andy Holgate got me smiling again, and the second climb of Sheep House Lane went well.

The third lap was when I started to feel the burn. Due to my knee issues, I'd never cycled more than about 75 miles before Ironman, so the last lap of this 112 mile ride was literally unknown territory. My average speed came down, climbs became more difficult (hello, bottom gear), and I felt the first twinges of nausea from all the energy bars, drinks, and the several gels I'd taken. But the support got me around, and I was chuffed to be able to finish Sheep House Lane for the third time without pushing my bike (there were a few walkers by then). I was also pretty pleased to see some expensive bikes passing me on this third lap. I might only have an entry-level aluminium beast, but I love my Giant, and it had kept me ahead of these £3,000 beauties for a good portion of the bike course. Nice.

The third lap went on ... and on ... and on, so much so that I had to really concentrate to make sure I hadn't done another lap by mistake. That's a stupid idea, but racing to this intensity does funny things to your sense of reasoning, and for a few troubling minutes I had to wonder.

But no. The turn for transition came—there were far fewer people on the green now—and a few miles later I rolled into T2. I almost fell over when I got off my bike, my legs were so shaky. Other than one brief stop to pee, I'd been in the saddle for seven-and-a-half hour.

I took off those horrible bikes shoes to walk to the changing hall. Luxury...

Run

I spent 13 minutes in T2 (too long, Timbo ... could do better!), eating fruit & nut mix, chatting with fellow competitors, changing my socks (what a treat!), making sure I was ready for the run. I was feeling GOOD! Over 9 hours of racing done, and I felt relatively fresh and eager to hit the road. The only worry ... my knee. It had given only a few light twinges during the bike, but I knew that the run would be the big challenge.

I started off taking it easy for the first couple of miles. I wanted to use my Garmin simply for pacing, but the bastard thing didn't pick up a satellite for the first 3 miles (again ... don't rely on tech). I didn't worry too much, though. I was used to running by feel, and I was enjoying being on my feet for the first time in 9 hours. I took it easy, chatting with a lady called Claire from Bristol who was also doing her first Ironman. It was great being able to talk with someone again, it's very difficult to do on the bike, and you're constantly aware of the non-drafting rules which makes it impossible to ride side by side. The human contact now was very welcome!

I felt good, and my knee was behaving itself. But I wasn't going to relax until at least the halfway point.

The run into town was nice, taking in some canal towpath and a few quieter roads. I settled into a steady rhythm, aiming for between 9:30 and 10:00 minute miles. I know that's nothing impressive, but it seemed the most sensible plan, and I wanted to stick to it. *Keep to your race plan!* I'd been told, and other than the slower-than-hoped-for bike, it was working.

Hitting the first lap of the run in and out of Bolton town centre sent a tingle down my spine. The support was *massive*, all along this 3 mile stretch of road (after the run in, there were three-and-a-half laps back and forth before the finish). People shouted and cheered, and with my Pirate top now on view (I'd biked in my NEWT cycling top) I lost count of the number of "Go Pirate!" or "Aargh!"s I got. Great, encouraging, humbling. The Pirates are a fantastic group of people (check out the Pirate Ship of Fools online), and it was wonderful having so much support from both spectators and runners alike.

And then ahead of me I saw my buddy Andy B! Andy had been pretty certain that he'd clock a 2 hour swim, so I'd just assumed I was ahead of him. Turns out he did a 1:42 swim––only a little slower than me––so somewhere on the bike course he must have passed me. I just can't think where! I caught up and we ran together for a bit, chatting, both now confident that by the end of the day we'd be Ironmen. But that was still hours away.

The feed stations had Mini Cheddars. I can't tell you how welcome they were after a day of Powerbars, gels, and bananas. I scooped them by the handful, coughing out loads of crumbs and having to double back for another drink. But still ... nice.

And then came a highpoint of the day (actually *two high points*, very close together). Andy Holgate was waiting at the bottom of the slight descent into the town centre, screaming me down, high-fiving, and the man's enthusiasm is palpable. He loves this sport. And even though he was largely responsible for me being there, I didn't even punch him. There were still two laps to go, though.

And then I saw my family. That was lovely. They were at the railing where 1000s lined the route through the town centre, and I ran over and gave my wife a kiss (probably sweating and sticky from gels etc, sorry babe), and ruffled my kids' hair, then I was off again, just a little bit emotional but with spirits lifted.

Next came the hardest part of the run. As well as being supported by thousands, the turnaround was behind the town hall, and I could hear people finishing.

That was tough.

I could see people running in towards the finish wearing their three coloured armbands (each signifying the completion of a lap) and hear the commentator and the roar of the crowd, and I still had about 15 miles to go. It was brutal. But it drew me on, and I ran back out of town on a high.

There was a brass band, a music station set-up, dancers, bagpipes, drinkers outside pubs, people camped outside their homes with barbecues and beer, family supporters ... so many people, all loving the day and cheering on the athletes. It was amazing, and I'd never experienced anything like it before. It kept my spirits up throughout the run, and even when my energy was flagging and it started to really, really hurt, the crowds pulled me on.

Second lap done—I'd seen a screaming Andy Holgate and my wife and kids again, good moments—and then I was into the final 6 miles. I was hurting, tiring, but feeling *great*! I'd managed to run the bulk of the marathon (by the end I reckon I'd run 23 out of the 26 miles, walking feed stations and that slight hill up out of town, and I'm delighted with that.) I was tired but determined. My legs were aching like hell, but my knee wasn't too bad. It was saying, 'Hey, Tim, I'm here, and tomorrow you're going to know it.' But it didn't scream at me on the day, and that's what counted.

That last lap was just incredible. I'd dreamed about it, both awake and asleep. I ran it all, loving every minute, and getting a bit choked when I thought, *This is it, I'm running towards the finish, I'm going to be an Ironman.* The last year had all converged towards this precise moment, and running back into the town centre for the last time, someone from the crowd shouted at me, "Milk it!"

I ran into the dogleg that led to the finish. Crowds were screaming. I was grinning. The commentator's voice welcomed racers in, though the whole finish area was still hidden behind the massive truck that held the big screen. And then at the one point where there weren't many people I saw Andy Holgate again. He was shouting me on, and I'm not sure what I said in reply. I think it was something like, "This is brilliant, I've done it, it's great!" I wasn't the mess of tears I thought I'd be, I think the excitement was just too high. I ran past him and turned into the finishing chute.

I pointed at my number and the commentator shouted, "And here's another one of the Pirates. *Tim, you are an Ironman!*"

There they were; those words.

I jogged down the red carpet, arms aloft, looking around to see if I could see Tracey and the kids. I didn't—the crowds were big, lining the Town Hall steps on one side and the grandstand on the other—but I knew they'd be there.

I crossed the line in 14 hours 12 minutes. That was it. Ironman.

I've bloody done it.

Afterwards

Medal, finisher's photo, then into the recovery tent for ... PIZZA! That was the best pizza I have ever tasted. There was also cake, melon, and water. I picked up my tee shirt and went to change, eager to see my family again. Changing was fun. I almost fell over a few times, but although my body was weakened, muscles shutting down, legs already stiffening, I felt bloody fabulous.

Outside, the first person I bumped into was Andy H. We swapped a sweaty hug, sorry Andy. Then my family found me, and we had a big hug and a kiss, and I'd done it. But I was still buzzing, and Andy B had yet to finish! I bought a coffee the size of a family car, and we went back into the grandstand and waited, and cheered Andy in. What a finish!

We all waited there together right until the end, watching everyone else finish including the last finisher, Steve. The poor guy was suffering badly, barely able to walk, and he finished something like ten minutes after the cut-off. But I still think they gave him a medal and called him Ironman, because he was. That was utter determination and bravery.

We returned to the hotel, and Tracey had bought me a couple of beers. Bless her. So at midnight she had to help me in and out of the shower because of my stiff legs and tiredness (and it's funny how chafing only makes itself known in a hot shower following a race), and the four of us sat up for a while, chatting, my wife and I having a drink, and it was just about the best finish to the best day ever.

Ex-chubby bloke, ex-unfit bloke, now an Ironman. Bloody hell.

As I fell asleep, I was already thinking about what next year might bring.

AND A SMALL POINT HERE, which you can take as advice if you like. The day after the race we drove to the Expo so that I could spend lots of money on 'finisher' kit. We had my bike on top of the car. When we entered the car park, under low height-restricted barriers, ignoring a parking attendant waving frantically, the bike was no longer on top of the car. So yes, watch out for those low car park barriers, eh?

I cannot mention here who was driving the car, because I love her too much for that. But it wasn't me. And my kids were nine and fourteen. And the only other person with us was my wife.

Crunch!

PART II

A WAY OF LIFE

"Don't be shit."

--common encouragement before a tough triathlon

7

FITNESS AS A BY-PRODUCT OF ABNORMAL BEHAVIOUR

I was enjoying feeling fitter and looking trimmer, despite having the occasional 'you need to put some more meat on your bones' comments from some family and friends. I never really understood this. Honestly, I've never been 'ripped'. Throughout my forties I've still always enjoyed food and a few drinks, so I never really trimmed down to racing snake status. At least, I don't think I did. I guess those comments came from people who'd known me as 'comfortable'––wearing a few extra pounds, carrying some middle-age padding––and seeing me with a thinner face ('drawn and haggard', some might say, and it's true, I have developed a few more lines) and contours not previously visible on my body might even have surprised some people (I've already told you about my relative who thought I was ill). But honestly, I don't think I went too extreme with the weight loss. Because of cake. And I'm sure my wife would agree. Although Tracey does still comment that my ass is too saggy and 'not there' enough, and that my shoulder is too bony for her to rest her head on.

I never really went in for the whole diet fad. I'd tried

before, in my thirties when I knew I needed to lose a few pounds, but ... I just like food too much. And a few beers here and there. Writing this now, I'm 51 years old and hovering around an average weight of 12st 4lbs (172 lbs). That's over two stones lighter than I was ten years ago when I started getting fit, and it's become my comfortable weight. In fact if I input my stats to a BMI calculator I'm still officially *overweight*! (I do have issues with the whole BMI thing as it doesn't take muscle mass or build into account at all). I eat and drink exactly what I want, although I do consider healthy food more than I did ten years ago, for sure. I've been vegetarian for about a year now (pescatarian I guess, I have a bit of salmon every month or so), but I still love cake and have a sweet tooth, and I enjoy a glass of wine and a real ale. So I really think my body has found its level, and my metabolism has settled around the exercise I do. It has truly become a way of life.

As I write this, it's October 2020. It's been a pretty shitty year, with the Covid-19 pandemic changing things for everyone. My training has continued throughout the pandemic, and indeed during lockdown I was getting out most days for a run or a bike ride. Swimming has been intermittent, and I went 5 months without swimming at all. But none of this exercise has been extreme, at least not in relation to what I'd normally be doing if this were a normal year with races and targets and training plans. I do understand that to many, the level of training I'm used to is often regarded as abnormal behaviour––I've still been doing 40 or 50 miles bikes rides at weekends through the summer––but for me, this year's training has been pretty gentle, and I'm quite happy with that. 2020 has been decidedly crap, but it's also been a year of calmer training, when I've been biking and running, and now swimming, to my own targets, and taking a lot of pleasure in all of it.

Maybe that's another way of saying I've become a bit of a lazy bastard and need to up my game, but next year we'll see. Next year, I have plans, more of which towards the end of this book.

And despite all that, with no races this year and a more casual approach to exercise, I *still* don't do all this stuff to keep fit. I do it because I *love* it. There's nothing quite like a trail run on the Blorenge on a Sunday morning, and sometimes I manage to get up there early when morning mists are still rising, and I'll do 7 miles and not see another soul. Sheep, yes. But no people. And a long bike ride in the autumn sun with a coffee and cake stop halfway is one of my favourite things to do.

So it's enjoyment. It's a way of life. And a lovely by-product of doing what I love is maintaining a decent level of fitness and getting down to a sensible weight.

Win-win? I bloody think so!

Fitness as a consequence of something you love, not a prime aim, is the greatest way to *get* fit. And it's the easiest way to *stay* fit.

It's also the best way to lose weight and keep it off. Don't go on a diet to lose weight, find something energetic that you develop a love for, and you'll lose weight as a consequence of doing this (alongside a healthier eating plan ... run every day but drink ten pints each night and eat burgers for three meals a day and the results won't be favourable). For some people it's zumba or dancing, running or swimming, hill walking or football. I'm not convinced that a large proportion of people succeed in losing weight simply because they love losing weight. They do it because they love the route they find getting there.

Fad diets come and go, and I often see them talked about on TV or social media. It's big business, and it can seem so cynical. For weeks before Christmas, advertising hits us will all the gorgeous rich food and booze we should be imbibing. We'll miss out if we don't eat that brand of sausage roll with delicately spiced pickle! We must be drinking this specially brewed craft beer! Because it's Chriiiiiiiiistmaaaaaaaaaas!

Then on Christmas afternoon, when the nation is crashed out in front of the TV in a food coma with their arteries making creaking noises to echo the whine from the overpacked dishwasher? Diet schemes! Weight loss programmes! Fatten them up, then lead them to the slaughter. It's commerce, I know. But it's also cynical and frustrating, and I'm delighted to now launch my own Tim-Plan Diet:

Ready? This'll change your life...

Eat healthier, and find something you love to make you move more!

There. Job done. That's five hundred pounds please. My invoice is in the mail.

That's what worked for me, anyway. But I'm not the boss of you.

8

PUSHING HARDER

A SELECTION OF OTHER RACES I'VE ENJOYED, AND LESSONS
LEARNED FROM THEM

You can do one Ironman and then sit back, proud
of what you've done but also acknowledging the
sheer ridiculousness of it, and that's fine because
as the saying goes 'pain is temporary, bragging rights last
forever', and even if you 'only' do one then you've still
pushed yourself hard, got fit, and done something that you
probably thought was impossible, and that most people you
tell about will think is a good indicator that you need your
head examined...

Or, you keep doing them.

I had well and truly caught the bug, and just a couple of
months after my first Ironman I signed up for Ironman
Wales in 2014. Destiny meant that I wouldn't end up racing
it––more about that soon––but in the meantime, it wasn't
just about doing Ironman races! And although through my
40s it was mostly long distance triathlon that became a large
part of my focus in exercise and training, this book's not just
about that. Because I ended up doing lots of other races and
adventures––shorter triathlons, marathons, bike sportives––
and I'd like to chat about a few of them here.

It's good to vary training and exercise, mentally and physiologically. Triathlon is naturally varied anyway, but you can still get caught up in specific distances and training patterns. That's great for some people, and I have very good friends who focus on certain races and distances, but usually that's because they're what I call Real Athletes, and they're looking for qualification or the podium. I'm at peace with the idea that this will probably never be me, and again it's back to that enjoyment thing—yes, I should run on the road to train for an Ironman that has a lapped road run, but I bloody love trail running!

So through my 40s I've been mixing it up quite a bit, and here's a selection of just a few races or events I've enjoyed competing in since getting fitter and finding my passion. And dotted here and there, a few tips and bits of advice I picked up on the way.

(Due to my excessively bad memory—it takes me a good fifteen minutes each morning to remember just who I am, where I am, and what the hell I'm *doing* here—I can't guarantee that the dates, or even the years of these events are correct. But they're bound to be there within a decade or two.)

Lakeland Trails Marathon—July 2012

Even whilst training for my first marathon I discovered that I preferred trail running to road running. So very soon after running the North Dorset race (road) I spent an evening on the internet searching for a trail run. Good sense would have dictated I find one within a reasonable distance, but who ever said I had good sense? Just ask my wife. And so it was I entered the Lakeland Trails Marathon, one whole lap of Coniston in the Lake District, just 10 weeks after my first.

After being plagued by terrible legs cramps during the North Dorset race (*Dickhead* –– going out too fast, not hydrating enough, paid the price in pain etc etc), I was determined that this one would go better. I was using salt tablets, made sure I hydrated well the days before the race, and I was very careful to watch my pace.

That's another thing I like about trail running. It's not so much about time and pace––hitting that eight-minute mile consistently, finishing a marathon sub-four hours––but getting up that next hill, picking the best route across that peat bog, dodging sheep and cows and groups of feral hikers, and not getting lost and breaking your ankle on a rock and dying in wretched pain and hunger in the lonely wilderness.*

(*most races are pretty good at sweeping up slow and lost runners)

This was a really beautiful race. The landscape was gorgeous, the weather was good––even in July in the Lakes, you should expect sun and rain and snow and meteor show-ers––and I ran a great race. My finishing time was some-where over five hours, but the route was largely off-road, and there really was a peat bog across the top of one of those hills. I popped salt tablets every hour and Jelly Babies every mile, and kept myself well hydrated. The views were glorious, the tee shirt is great because it says 'Survivor' rather than just splashing the race name, and I had the best burger and real coffee from a van at the end of the race. It was so good that the burger van guy was walking around asking everyone if they were enjoying their burger––he was a portly gentleman, obviously partaking of his own produce, which in itself is a good sign. I can still taste them now, and I've become a veggie!

After the race I made an interesting discovery in the

showers (stop sniggering at the back)—you'll often only discover chafing when you're showering afterwards. I do recall letting out a little yelp, and soon after I sat outside with another coffee and called Tracey to tell her how it went.

"So how was it?"

"Yes, loads of fun, all good. The old boy's a bit chafed though."

In the background I heard my daughter saying: "What, Grandad Peter?"

It was a ridiculously long way to go for a marathon. Up in one day, marathon and six hour drive home the next day. But it was nine years ago now, and I can still remember much of the race, which shows it was a good one.

Recommended. But don't forget the chafing cream.

Blaenafon Triathlon—2013

It's a pretty good indication of the types of races I prefer that I entered this as probably my third or fourth triathlon. This was a few months before Ironman UK. It's a local race (I can literally run the few miles to the leisure centre where it was held), and at the time was famed for being the longest running triathlon in the UK. This first time for me was their 30th anniversary, which made for a special race and, much more importantly, a fucking huge cake at the celebration meal afterwards.

After finishing this race I said two things. Thing One was, "I'm never, ever doing this race again." Thing Two was, "If I can do the Blaenafon Triathlon, I can do anything." I lied to myself about Thing One and raced it two more times in the following few years, but when I said those words— convulsing on the grass close to the finish like a deer taken out by a marksman, trying to catch my breath, begging someone to chop off my legs because that would hurt less— I really meant them.

And Thing Two really helped me later that year at Ironman UK. Because it's true ... if you can race Blaenafon, you can do anything.

But first, an interesting aside...

Years before I started exercising, probably in my chubby thirties when the most exercise I did was a brisk walk and three miles on a twenty-year-old bike, I was in Pontypool Park with my wife and very young kids when this race was on. I remember seeing the run route along the long path out of the park lined with bollards and tape (this long path was the bike in and run out route), and watching those lanky, skinny men and women clad in figure-hugging lycra sweating blood and pleading with local dog walkers to please put them out of their misery, and thinking, *Crazy bloody idiots, what the hell do they think they're doing?* I had no real concept of triathlon at the time, and these people looked almost alien to me. Owned many ball-sacks, Yoda did.

Years later, by the time I started the run clad in figure hugging lycra and sweating blood, I was pleading with passers-by to put me out of my misery.

So, the race. A quick run-down: it was a quirky distance, with an 800 metre pool swim, 28 mile-ish bike, and the run maybe 8 or 9 miles, mostly off-road. So not far, right? Easy?

No.

The pool swim wasn't fun. Horrible. Get that out of the way, 800m of misery when I was either too slow and getting overtaken, or thought I was too fast and overtook someone only to discover I'm not that fast at all and I was actually drafting them pretty well and that was a lesson learned, right there.

Out onto the bike course. Or should I call it, Twenty Eight Miles Of Hell. Oh, sure, it started fine, with a gentle warm-up then a nice downhill and flat bimble along a dual-carriageway. And then it started to gets bumpy.

The ride took in two epic climbs. The first, Oak Lane, is the Grown Up version of the dreaded Tumble climb. They're the same elevation and reach the same place––the top of the Blorenge, one of the three lovely mountains surrounding Abergavenny––but Oak Lane is the route you take if you really fancy yourself as a climber on the bike. Or if you're one of the sadistic organisers of the Blaenafon Triathlon.

The road surface was terrible. The tarmac was potted, bits of the banks on either side of the road had fallen, dishing out slicks of mud and stones across the road. And it was so twisty that even if you *could* manage to find some sort of a rhythm ... you *couldn't*. A really tough climb, with one section that hits over 20% for about 200 metres. Scorcher.

Oh, but hang on, it wasn't over yet. Because once you'd hit the top of the Blorenge and rescued your lungs from atop your shoulders as if a rogue band of Vikings had performed the Blood Eagle ceremony on you somewhere on that 20% climb, and you'd done that nice downhill into Blaenafon, you were faced with the second tough climb of this race.

The British. This hill might not have offered quite the climbing distance, but it was tougher than Oak Lane for several reasons.

First, the road surface in places was terrible, and made Oak Lane's cracked and potted tarmac look like the polished surface of one of the mirrors in the Hubble telescope. Except less shiny, and not in orbit.

Second, I already had the ascent of the Blorenge in my legs, and I'd had that long sweeping descent into town to lull my muscles into a false sense of security. Then this hill reared up and smacked me in the face.

Third, it felt all the more remote and desolate. The bottom of the climb was haunted by bands of marauding youths on quad bikes, who most definitely didn't intend letting me pass as they rode downhill four abreast and I struggled uphill in granny gear ... at that level of *This is hurting* that means if you have to stop, you'll have real trouble starting uphill again. I did manage to slip through between them without being kicked off my bike or mugged, but a friend of mine also encountered these reprobates after me, and he ended up having to jump off his bike and face up to them. His triathlon became a quadrathlon, with an almost-fight thrown in. Not good. Bet their parents are proud.*

(*Actually, probably are.)

British done, the descent was a mixture of fallen branches, potholes that resembled small surface-mining systems, and suicidal sheep.

Then it was a long, fast ride back to transition. *Ahh*, you might think, *all the tough hills are done now. It's just the run left. Nearly finished.*

And the run started quite easy with a couple of miles along the picturesque canal towpath before hitting the muddy, rocky hills again. I love trail running, but usually prefer a trail to run along, not a quagmire.*

(*At this point in the race I had to remind myself, *I'm doing this for fun.* I've said this to myself a lot, at least once in virtually every race I've ever done. In this race I said it half a dozen times, and never once believed it.)

Stumbling downhill through Pontypool Park towards

the finish line, I thought of those competitors I'd been watching years ago thinking *They must be mad*, and realised how right I'd been back then. I crossed the line in a time of ... I don't know, seven days? A week and a half? It didn't matter, this was the Blaenafon Triathlon! My wife was there to cheer me across, and was also there with a bottle of water when I hit the grass and just lay there for a bit, trying to remember my name and which century I'd been born in and how breathing worked.

"Never again," I said. "I'm never doing this again. It's mad. It's horrible. Never again." *

(* I did the race again the following year, and again a couple of years later when it moved to Abergavenny and the bike ride took in the Tumble and Llangynydr and the run was to the top of the Sugarloaf Mountain and back down...)

I then hobbled to the shower, changed, and went up to the celebratory meal and award-ceremony––why are these things always upstairs?––and had a pint of Guinness, and ate cake.

Yes, it was hard, but I stand by what I said––If you can do Blaenafon, you can do anything. It's nowhere near as long as an Ironman, but it's unrelentingly tough, both physically and mentally. I do wonder if those youths on quad bikes were actually paid by the organisers. It's a huge mental boost doing a race like this, and as you'll see soon I continued looking for the more unusual, quirky, and tough races, as well as the occasional fast flat events designed for racing snakes.

This became one of my favourite races. I love the razzamatazz of Ironman, the streets lined with supporters cheering you on, but I love even more these grass roots events, where often it's just you against the race. I'll talk about this a bit more later, when I tell you about my adventures racing The Brutal.

Yes, I chose a race with that name. Go figure.

Tour of Pembrokeshire—2014

So let's do a bike sportive, shall we? Easy, right? Just a bimble in the sun?

With the Blaenafon Triathlon, my first couple of marathons, and Ironman UK under my belt, I never believed a mere bike race ("But it's a sportive!" I hear the organisers cry, "Not a race!", and yeah, they're right, but show me a triathlete who doesn't compare times after a sportive and I'll show you a poor dentist) would challenge me as much as this one.

Pembrokeshire is hilly. There was one hill on this route, short but very steep, where most riders zig-zagged to actually get up. And the weather was horrible—windy, raining, cold, I almost got blown off several times, and not in a good way. Riding up and down country lanes with gale-force winds blowing, you become very aware of where the gate opening are. I saw several cyclists blown right across the road, and I'm sure a few ended up in the ditch.

It's also a matter of meteorological curiosity how, when its windy, it's always a head wind on the bike, no matter which direction you're cycling in. There should be papers done on this. Where's Michael Fish when you need him?

I'd intended doing the long ride, partly because it was another night away from home so I wanted to make the most of being away. I think the long ride was about 100 miles, and when I reached the point where I could peel off for the 70 mile route I sat there for a bit, considering. I think this was about 40 miles into the ride. Usually I'd go for the tougher option, but with a feeling of subtle failure pecking at me I took the shorter route.

I was glad I did. By the end of the ride I could hardly recall which language I spoke, and this is one of the few events where I had to have a good sit down afterwards, refuelling with chips and coffee and cake, and have a good long think.

I mean, what the bloody hell? I actually felt traumatised. This was a tough one, for sure, and character building. I remember calling my wife from the car park and saying I'd have to wait an hour before starting to drive home, and then on the way I stopped for a Costa and fell asleep in one of their (not very comfortable) chairs.

Didn't even get a medal! I had a wooden coaster instead, and I'm looking at it right now. That four-inch square of wood was well earned.

Titan Triathlon—2016

This was a middle distance (half-iron distance) training race for Ironman Wales. I chose it because it's close, distinctly hilly, and very scenic. It's held in the excellent Parc Bryn Bach facility, a great place for a race base, and it's gruelling from start to finish.

The swim is in the lake which is the central attraction for the facility—they do all manner of water sports as well as swimming, and it's a fishing lake too. It's also home to many, many ducks and geese, so one of the big challenges pre-swim is trying to get into the water without tripping over an impressively large goose turd.

It's a deep water start, so lots of fun with elbows in your ribs and feet in your face. I've grown to enjoy the washing machine start, and my 2-lap swim was quite fun, especially hauling myself through masses of lake weeds. That really upset some people, but for me it's all part of the fun of open water swimming.*

(*see Ironman Wales report for further open water swimming fun, including punching giant jellyfish in the face (or arse ... who the hell knows?), front-crawling through vomit, and other delights).

It was a warm day to race, and I made sure I was stocked up with enough water and gels for the bike. This was a really tough bike course, starting with a gently rolling approach to Llangynydr hill. The descent was very fast, so fast that I rode the brakes half of the way. Scary! The rest of the bike was along mostly-familiar roads, apart from one short, really steep hill out near Brecon where I saw one guy whose crank had snapped from his TT bike.

Then it was back ... and ready for that Llangynydr ascent. It's a tough hill this one, much harder than the Tumble (which is the famous ascent of the Blorenge mountain), as it has a couple of false summits where it's easy to think, *Yay, finished!* Nope, you haven't.

This was where I bumped into a guy called Jon, who became my hill buddy. We rode up that horrible hill together, chatting when we could draw a breath, keeping each other going, and it's definitely true that a distraction can make something like this seem easier. Of course, if you're racing a branded Ironman and you're doing this, a motorcycle ref will likely drag you to the side of the road and ritually execute you, because it's probably classed as drafting. But it worked well for us here, and with the end of the bike ride in sight Jon moved on ahead. We'd see each other on the run, and he was way ahead of me (turns out I shouldn't have felt bad about this ... soon after he ran a half-marathon every day for a month for charity, so, you know. Real Athlete).

I was glad to get off the bike. Great, only a half marathon left! It was deceptively hilly and hot, but I finished the race and grabbed a terrific race tee-shirt and medal, and coffee, and the inevitable cake. A superb event, and brilliant prep for Ironman Wales.

May the Fourth Be With You marathon—2016

You might want to file this one under Races I Did For The Bling. The medal is the size of a dinner plate, and features all the familiar Star Wars characters in undoubtedly lawsuit-attracting poses, should Disney get wind of it. Also useful as a car jack, or a deadly weapon should you get into a tussle on the way home from the race.*

(*This didn't happen, but if it had I'd have won.)

The race was held on May the fourth (from memory, a Tuesday), which is Star Wars day. No, I'm not going to explain it. You either get it or you don't, and frankly if you don't then the Force is not strong with you, and may you end up getting roasted and eaten by rabid Ewoks.

This was another trail marathon, another exercise in horribleness, but run in the gorgeous Shropshire hills. Just forty minutes for me by train, this was a lovely race, nicely organised by How Hard Can It Be Events (answer: very). Scenic, challenging, the toughest part for me was halfway through when I ended up back at the start and race base ... and saw all the half-marathoners collapsing in gibbering sweating heaps while helpers brought them food and water and medical aid, and us full marathoners had to turn around and *do it all again*!

I did learn something here––you can carry too little

water, but never too much. I ran out of water between two aid stations that were several miles apart on the remotest part of the run, and it was a hot sunny day in them hills! Luckily I ended up running with a guy who lent me a small water bottle from his vest, so I managed to make it to the next aid station without dehydrating and melting away like that evil Nazi in *Raiders of the Lost Ark*.

The train journey home was fun, as I had the entire table and four seats to myself. No idea why.*

(*I hadn't had a chance to change and was sweaty, muddy, and my trainers stank of sheep shit).

Brilliant. And in writing this I notice it's on again in 2021. This *is* the race I'm looking for.

There are loads more races I could write about, but I'm going to pick just a few more of the more enjoyable, unusual ones:

Long Course Weekend, Tenby––this is a brilliant weekend with Iron distance racing split over three days (2.4 mile sea swim Friday, 112 mile bike Saturday, marathon on Sunday, and then beer and cake). I'm doing the whole thing in 2021 (more about my 2021 plans at the end of this book), but previously I did the full swim and full bike, but not the marathon because of a dodgy knee.

On the bike, halfway up Wiseman's Bridge on my final lap (so I guess just a few miles out of Tenby) my chain snapped. Bollocks! But this was a good thing, because it taught me several things. First, being shortsighted and wearing contact lenses in a race means you can't see things close-up, so to change a tyre or fix a mechanical is doubly hard. Second, if you know your bike is cranky before a race, get it checked over. Third, if the bike mechanics say they'll drive you to the finish, you can put your foot down with them. I told them I wanted to finish on my own, so the great guys turned my chain around, removed a couple of broken links, and I limped in to the finish covered in oil and really, really, really ready for a recovery pasty.*

(*Yes, this is an Actual Thing).

Immortal Half, Stourhead––such a scenic race with its base in a beautiful country manor, this events taught me that if you're suffering on the run and don't feel you should slow down when you pass a mate to talk in case you can't start again ... you shouldn't slow down to talk to a mate you've passed, because you won't be able to start again.

Cotswold 113/Classic––I've raced this one several times, including in a couple of relays, and I just love it. It's become one of the NEWT's club races because it's local-ish and so well organised by the 113 Events team. It's flat and fast, apart from one very subtle hill on the bike that feels like Everest after you've smashed out 20 fast miles. A terrific race, thoroughly recommended.

Brutal Half, 2017––Yes, it's called the Brutal. There's a clue there somewhere. As with the Blaenafon Triathlon, this is a tough, rural, small race that quickly became my favourite, and part of a series put on by Brutal Events. And because I loved it so much––and actually performed pretty well, finishing in 26th place out of 74 men––I entered the full Brutal for 2018. I talk about that stunning race later, so I won't say much more here other than ... the name is very appropriate.

Fan Dance 2020––This was my only race of 2020, thanks to Covid. My friend Lyndon from the club invited me to join him, and what an adventure it was. The Fan Dance is run by ex-Special Forces and takes place on the same route as part of the SAS selection training, up and over Pen-y-Fan (the tallest mountain in South Wales) ... twice. We opted for the clean fatigues entry, meaning that we wouldn't have to carry a heavy bergen, but that in no way made it easier, as clean fatigues means you end up running as much of it as you can. It was cold and a bit snowy, but in comparison to other years we had it easy. They stress that they run the race in all but the direst conditions. It was about 14 miles with over 3,000 feet of climbing, and it was truly character building. The sort of race I hate and love at the same time. I'll do it again one day.

9

IT'S ALL ABOUT THE KIT

N o it isn't.

But sometimes it is.

Let me explain.

A good friend of mine in my triathlon club—someone who's pretty much a pro-level triathlete, who has qualified for Kona, won major races, goes sub-9 hours for an Ironman, and whose accomplishments I find pretty mind-blowing—once told me how much he'd spent on a set of pedals. And they cost more than my bike.

For this particular Real Athlete that expenditure was perfectly justified. If those ultra-light perfectly stiffened intricately sized carbon pedals gained him, say, a minute on an Ironman bike ride through weight difference and power transference, that could easily be the difference between a podium place or not, a Kona qualification or not. If I spent all that money on a set of pedals and gained a minute or two, it might be the difference between 865th place and 832nd.

Problem is, a lot of advertising is aimed at the pointy end

of the field, and a lot of people not at the pointy end buy this expensive kit thinking it's essential, or will help them go faster, or it's just the stuff to be seen wearing/riding/swimming in. I'm not saying it's a bad thing spending a lot of money on kit. Er ... I've done it. Triathlon can be a very expensive hobby, if you let it run away with you. But for someone like me––distinctly middle of the pack or, as I usually aim for, upper half of finishing field and anything higher than that and I'm well happy––it's a long way from essential.

Over the past decade I've subscribed to *Runner's Magazine, Trail Running Magazine, Outdoor Fitness,* and *Triathlon 220.* All great magazines, and I still pick them all up from time to time. I even once had a feature on me in Outdoor Fitness! It was to do with a thriller novel I had out, *The Hunt,* which was heavily influenced by my love of endurance sport and training in the mountains. Although I've never been shot at whilst running. And this resulted in the only time I've ever been recognised in public as a writer, when a guy in T2 at the Immortal Half Ironman race said, 'Hey, you're the writer guy from Outdoor Fitness!' We stopped and had a quick chat, and therefore he is entirely to blame for me not winning that race.

But I digress.

So, these magazines are great, but more often than not I found that many of the adverts, and often the gear reviews, tended towards the more expensive side. I know, advertising, earning money, and it's all about the bucks. But I've never bought a showerproof jacket for £170. About 8 years ago I bought two RonHill showerproof jackets, one black and one hi-viz, for about £25 each, and I've only just had to throw one of them away because it's worn thin and torn through use. I've found them both really useful on the bike, and though they screw up to the size of your fist or smaller, they've always been *perfect* for chilly days running in the hills. Running shorts, too, can sometimes edge into three figures, but the best pair I've ever owned are a RonHill pair (I see a pattern here), that cost me around £30. Comfortable, with a compression short inside that prevents chafing, I still use them now even though they're faded through use and washing. As for cycling gear, yes, I've spent £70 on a pair of bib shorts, but they were club-branded NEWT gear. And I have spent £100 on a race suit (a sort of second skin tri suit, branded in NEWT club colours, which you can wear from the first moment of a race to the last and which feels like you're not wearing anything ... and frankly, it can look like it sometimes too, so be mindful of where you 'place' yourselves when you dress, gents).

But no, I've never spent £70 on a running tee shirt. In fact, I think I've only ever bought two or three running tee shirts, because *you don't have to buy them at all!* I've got drawers full of race tee shirts that I use for training. And of course, a select few of these tee shirts are kept back for casual wear.*

(*Bragging rights).

And here's another aside...

It's actually a very precise science trying to decide which tee or sweatshirt you wear to a race the day before when you're registering, racking your bike, or just hanging around the venue checking out transition and generally sizing up the competition from the corner of your eye. You have to be subtle, yet confident with your choice. Turn up at a supersprint triathlon rocking your Deca-Ironman tee might be overkill, but I think decent Olympic distance wear is allowable in these circumstances, and if you've got the build and racing chops I think you could push as far as middle distant. Likewise, turn up at the briefing for Ironman Wales wearing a sprint tri tee and you'll either be a) laughed at, gently and quietly, or b) you'll become something of a mystery, an enigma, and everyone will eye you as a Dark Horse and a potential race winner, having the confidence to sport such attire at this time.

Me, I usually bring out the big guns at long distance events. *Oh, you've done an Ironman, have you?* I mentally mutter, making sure they can see my Brutal Extreme Triathlons sweatshirt ('Pass the Weak, Hurdle the Dead').

So, back to the price of kit. I'm not saying you won't need to spend some money on decent race attire. I learned that the hard way, training for the Three Peaks in cotton tee shirts that, when loaded with sweat, gain the weight of a medium-sized farm animal and stretch down so that the neckline is approximately at waist level. You'll need proper kit suitable for your training—wicking material, hi-viz, comfortable, well-fitted so you're not chafed to buggery. But unless you do have money to throw away, it's not necessary to be drawn into the The-More-I-Spend-The-Faster-I'll-Be-And-The-Better-I'll-Look trap. Spend it if you've got it, sure. But you don't need to put yourself in debt or syphon cash from your family's 'Saving For A Holiday Of A Lifetime' pot.*

(*Our family's holiday of a lifetime was entirely built around an Ironman! See what I did there? Damn, I'm getting good at this. But more of that in Part Three).

And now the caveat. Because I *have* spent quite a bit of money on bikes. And this is why. I was once introduced to the formula that says:

Optimum number of bikes = N + 1 (where N is current number of bikes).

I'm not very good at mathematics, so I took this equation as gospel. I now own four bikes, which obviously is one less than the optimum number. That must be true. The formula says so.

My first bike, bought even before I got into triathlon and right at the beginning of my journey towards getting fit, was a cheapish mountain bike from Halfords. It was about £300 at the time, and I still use it now! I do very little serious mountain biking—I value my bones—although I keep thinking it's something I'd like to try some more. But until I do get more serious about it, this is a fun bike for a bit of muddy off-roading. It's rear suspension, heavy, and probably ridiculously out of date considering the speed of biking R&D, new designs, and new materials. But I've done a couple of off-road duathlons on it, and a race through Wentwood Forest called the Goshawk Challenge that was a real trial. My son uses the bike too, and it's been a lot of fun.

My second bike was my first road bike. As I was getting into triathlon I needed a road bike, so as mentioned before I walked into my local bike shop with £800 in cash. They smiled and offered me a coffee. But I was there to spend, and I didn't walk out of that shop, I *rode* out on a new Giant Defy 3 aluminium road bike with clip-in pedals, helmet, and other bits and pieces. I was the bee's knees on that thing. It was a bright white with black lettering, and compared to anything I'd ever ridden before, *swift!*

My first time out on this bike was a real surprise ... because when I looked down I realised I was riding nothing. This was my first ever time on a road bike, and in a year of 'first-evers' it was a great, though disconcerting experience, not looking down and seeing that meaty mountain bike beneath me. The tyres were so thin, the frame fine, the handles tight, and the whole thing felt so damn *delicate*. For the first couple of rides I was pretty nervous, but I soon got into it. It was just like riding a bike. I did my first few triathlons and first Ironman on that glorious aluminium steed, as well as a few tough sportives. I still have it, and my son rides it now. We had a nice few rides during the 2020 Covid lockdown, and it's good that it's still being used. Though I have to admit I've jumped back on it a couple of times and thought, *How the hell did I do an Ironman on this?*

Because a few years ago, loving triathlon more and more, feeling fitter ... and yes, lured by advertising, and fellow club-mates' lovely bikes ... I walked back into my local bike shop and told them what I was looking for. They smiled and offered me a coffee *and* a cake, and after a good chat I slapped down the cash for a new Giant Propel full-carbon aero road bike. This is my favourite bit of kit. It's a beauty, bright red with white lettering, aero brakes and frame, and I reckon I've ridden 12,000 miles on it racing and training. It cost me £1700 (along with regular servicing, new wheels, etc). I've raced loads of times on it, and it's always a pleasure to ride. My precioussssrs.

But that's not all.

Three years ago I had a Hollywood movie made out of one of my books (check out *The Silence* on Netflix, and see if you can pause it on my half-second cameo as a bloodied corpse that Stanley Tucci steps over). Waiting for news on something like this is nerve-wracking to say the least—there's no middle ground, either the film will happen and you'll get paid, or it won't and you won't—and when the deal finally dropped and I knew it as a certainty, I treated myself to something I'd had my eyes on for a while. A triathlon, or TT bike.

I'll admit right now that the bike I bought is too good for me. All the gear, no idea, that's me (a bit ... I do have *some* idea). It's a Canyon Speedmax CF8 and it cost me £2700. That's a big lump of money, but the bike is a work of art. If I didn't ride it I'd put it on the wall and stare at it. I'm not sure my wife would agree, but it's a beautiful machine, all attractive angles and every inch of the design given over to aero gains and speed. Best of all, it came in my triathlon club colours of black and yellow! It was fate, I tell you.

And then to spoil the whole design and look of the thing, there's me sitting in the saddle. So yes, it's probably far too good for me, but like I said it was a treat. I've raced it only a couple of times, and have trained on it in better weathers. But I'll admit here, and it's not something that comes easily—I prefer to ride my road bike. It's probably just time in the saddle, but the Canyon feels uncomfortable (yes I've had a pro bike fit), and I've never quite felt as safe on it as on the roadie. Probably because I fell off it once, chasing a Strava segment, and cracked a rib! If I hit a pothole it's really jarring on the shoulders and neck, and there's a confidence thing too ... I'll never hammer downhill at almost 50mph on the tri bars, because I need access to the brakes to make me feel safe and in control (the brakes on the tri bike are on the drop bars, and the tri bars where you rest down on your forearms have the gear changers).

But it's still a thing of beauty and it attracts appreciative glances when I'm out and about, and that's all that really matters.*

(*Of course it isn't.)

So, those are my bikes. I'm still one short, according to that special equation. And lately I've been thinking a Crosstrail bike might be a bit of fun for when the triathlon season ends.

Maybe I need another film deal.

A few more words about kit to finish off, and remember this––like everything in this book––is purely subjective. I am not a clothing model. I'm sure my wife would agree. I go with what I find comfortable, and I'll always look for a good price on kit. A £150 pair of trainers will almost certainly not make me any faster than a £60 pair, although hi-viz go-faster stripes might make it appear that way.

I had a gait analysis when I first started running and was pretty neutral. Ever since then I've used ASICS Cumulous shoes for road running. The first pair I bought were fine, and going on the basis of 'if it ain't broke don't fix it' I've stuck to these shoes ever since. I usually spend anything from £50 to £75, depending on time of year I buy and whether or not it's a new 'model' or not. Shoe suppliers spout all manner of design characteristics and trademarked special arch supports and lacing systems and sole structures with hexagonal support cells instead of octagonal, but really? I've honestly not ever taken much notice. If the shoe fits, and is comfortable, that's fine for me. Also, sometimes they're ridiculously colourful, so I figure I'll never get lost in the dark.

For trail shoes, which I buy more regularly, I used to go for Adidas Terrex but now also alternate with Salomon shoes. Again, it's often cost that I go by, and I always look at reviews too. I have wider feet, and tend to go a size up in both road and trail shoes, partly because of the spade-like feet anomaly in my family (we've all got big heads, too. What's going on?), but also to cater for swelling feet whilst running. I love a good pair of trail shoes, and there's nothing like getting a new flash pair covered in mud and cow shit after a crisp autumn run. Job done!

I think that's all I've got to say on kit. Other than to

mention that I read a scientific study suggesting that you *really do* go faster on a red bike, because of the psychological effect of knowing you're riding a red bike.

Even though my Giant road bike is red and bloody lovely, I can categorically state that this is not the case.

10

RACE REPORT:

OUTLAW TRIATHLON — 26TH JULY, 2015

I loved Ironman UK so much that soon after I signed up for Ironman Wales a year later, in 2014. Unfortunately I picked up a niggling knee injury, which in retrospect was probably the same that I'd had before IM UK (a small meniscus tear). I was determined to race, but my training wasn't quite where I wanted it. I threw my toys out of the pram, cancelling Ironman Wales and having a bit of a low period about it all. Apart from losing £200 (because Ironman really don't like you cancelling or pulling out of their races), my focus for the year went.

In retrospect, I'm pretty sure I could have raced. Which leads me on to talking about injuries, I guess. Another digression, and why not? This book isn't written to a strict plan, and like a triathlon training plan, some days you might just want to go off piste and do a run instead of a bike ride. So, before I hit the water at Nottingham for the Outlaw ... injuries.

When I started my long, sweaty, chafed and cake-rich journey towards (relative) fitness, I was very conscious of injuries. Or, more accurately, not getting them. Part of this stemmed from not having done stuff like this before, and probably an underlying concern about a) what I was doing to my body, and b) how a small injury might turn into something larger, thus preventing me from racing. The bigger the race you sign up for, the more pressure builds around it—training, preparation, the long physical and psychological lead-up, and the risk of everything coming crashing down if you pick up an injury. So I was careful, and probably a bit paranoid. If I had a twinge in my leg, I'd go to see the physio. A sore foot, and I'd spend an evening in ever-more doom-laden Googling, eventually deciding that my large toe had actually fallen off and my heel had become detached from the rest of my body and was happily sauntering off somewhere without me. Truth was, most of the time I was just picking up aches and pains instead of actual injuries. I once spent a *lot* of money with a shoulder specialist because I had painful shoulders. The sessions were so costly I stopped going, started swimming *more*, and the pain went away.

I'm not saying you should ignore potential injuries, because one of the most important tips I could give is, *Listen to your body.* It'll tell you when something's wrong, when you've been over-training, and when perhaps it's time for a day or two doing something gentler and different. But it is important to keep things in perspective, and learn to *understand* your body, so that you can differentiate between an actual injury, training aches, and something more serious. Back then I was definitely over-cautious, rushing to the physio with tweaks and twinges which now I'd ice and rest or roll out with a foam roller and continue training. Maybe it was no bad thing to be like this when I began, but it did really mean that I canned Ironman Wales when I probably didn't need to. But I would return in 2016 (see race report later).

In 2015, though, it was time for the Outlaw. This is an iron distance event not run by the Ironman organisation. One Step Beyond run it, and it's a terrific race, usually selling out very quickly every year (along with the middle distance Outlaw events they run ... I did this race in 2014). Athlete care is second to none, and the race takes place at the National Watersports Centre in Nottingham. It was really strange returning here. As I wrote earlier, when I was 15 I'd been into canoeing, and I'd come here to race with a couple of other club members. Maybe I should have learnt to swim back then, because I succeeded in completely capsizing before the start of my main race and I didn't get to compete. Epic Fail. I did race with someone else in a doubles K2, but our boat had a dodgy rudder and we came last. Epic Fail, part 2.

So it was strange seeing the building, the long rectangular lake, and the control/results tower again the day before the Outlaw triathlon kicked off here. Epic Fail #3 not required here...

I'd raced the Outlaw Half the year before so I was familiar with the set-up, and parts of the course. That gave me a bit of peace of mind the day before when my family and I arrived and I started getting my kit together. After buying a lovely tee shirt from a grumpy vendor...

"Will you be here tomorrow before the race?"

"Yes. At five a.m. Five."

I was delighted that my brother Nick agreed to come along for the day, watch me race, and take loads of photos. He loves photography and takes great snaps, and it's always good to have someone to cheer you on. It was also really nice that he lives in Melton Mowbray, so we crashed there the night before the race. Nice food, a pint, and a nervous night's 'sleep'.*

(*not.)

I was up and ready very early, along with Nick, leaving Tracey and our two kids to come along a bit later to see the start of the race. I checked my bike and kit, made a last toilet visit, then it was time to get suited up for my swim. Perfect timing. Nick wished me good luck and I told him that I'd be seeing him again, hopefully, in seven or eight hours once I was off the bike.

The water was fine, if a little stinky—there were lots of Geese there, and I'd meet them again later—and the weeds were a bit gross. But as each race came and went I was getting more used to the open water swim, and especially the mass start. It really troubles some people, but I actually now quite enjoy the bash and bump of a mass swim start. I think it's because it always signals the start of a race, and I really don't like all the early-morning 'hanging around in a wetsuit needing a pee being nervous looking at the weather wondering what kit I've forgotten' side of things... *

(*I've never forgotten any major kit, unlike a mate of mine who rocked up to an early morning race start without his bike helmet!)

And we were off! Pretty soon I got into my rhythm, a few strokes and sight, few strokes and sight. It's really hard to go much wrong on the Outlaw swim. The lake is long and rectangular, and the swim is up and back, the lake split in two by a line of buoys. So even if you do drift a little, it's tough to go too far out of true. Even when you're swimming into the rising sun!

I finished my swim in 1:15, a great time for me. I cut my toe exiting the water. I saw the blood as the wetsuit strippers (not nearly as much fun as they sound) told me to sit and ripped my wetsuit off, and then saw Tracey and my kids at a barrier cheering me on! My toe didn't hurt, but I had to mop up the blood while I changed, and the little cut would come back to haunt me on the bike.

The Outlaw bike is a really flat course, loop one, loop two, then loop one for the second time. It's not closed roads, but there are lots of controlled junctions and coned off sliproads onto and off from main roads. And I have to say, it was bloody cold! This was July, remember. But I learned here that you can't trust the weather in this country at any point, and out onto the bike I wore my tri top, a skin, and my bike jersey. I was glad I did. I passed one guy in just a sleeveless tri suit, he was shivering so much he couldn't stop his teeth from chattering, his hands were clawed around his hoods, and he said he was having trouble changing gear or using his brakes.

Two things I'd say here. First, it's stupid turning up at a race like this unprepared for troublesome weather. If you don't need that extra kit you can just leave it in transition, nothing lost. Second, how much time are you going to save by not chucking on another couple of layers? A minute? Big frigging deal, unless you're at the pointy end and that minute is the difference between a podium or not. And for 95% of people racing, that's not the case. And the third point of these two things I'd like to say ... I heard that people were pulling out of the bike leg because of the cold. So even if they did save themselves a minute, the rest of their race was a miserable cold-fest until they DNF'd and went home pissed off having wasted six months' training and their entry fee.

Numpties.

I think this might also have been the race when I came closest to seeing someone die. I've seen plenty of bike accidents—usually the results, not the accidents themselves—involving broken wheels and bloodied riders, sometimes with no obvious cause, often at the bottom of unfamiliar hills or tight bends. But this incident was pretty hair-raising (and I'm bald). A woman overtook me on the bike as we approached a roundabout (remember, this wasn't closed roads). She was belting it, race head on, and she powered out into the roundabout without slowing or looking where she was going. A screech of brakes, and her right pedal must have whispered along the bumper of the Range Rover that, somehow, didn't turn her into roadkill. It was a sobering sight. I'm always very careful on the bike, especially when racing. I've had a few spills, but only when cycling on my own, and only one of them significant (cracked rib). This, though ... no race is worth that, for you as an athlete and more importantly, for the poor bastard who might have to live with seeing you going under their wheels.

Take care out there, people.

So, back to the race! Loop 1 on the bike was country roads and relatively quiet. Loop 2 was a busier portion on larger roads, and I was glad to get that out of the way and swing back onto Loop 1 again. 112 miles later and I rolled back into T2 with a time of 6:19. Thrilled with that, and in fact this was looking to be a really fast race (for me ... and I only ever really race myself).

The run was tough. It was still cold when I began with a familiar, "Almost done now!" thought. Just a marathon to do! (*No, Lebbon, it's an Ironman run!*) My teeth were chattering, but it soon warmed up, even though rains came and went during my run. Mostly they were pretty welcome. I saw my brother Nick on the run out of transition and threw a few poses for his camera, then I was out onto the course. Like the bike route it's very flat, and I have to admit I found the lake lap pretty soul-destroying. Especially the first time. The lake is about 1.5 miles long, and when you round the top end and head back, the other end is barely visible. You see how far you have to go ... and that's not nice.

I tried a tactic I learned reading Chrissie Wellington's brilliant book *A Life Without Limits*. Chrissie is an Ironman legend, a lovely person, inspiring and passionate about our sport. So, her tactic for breaking up the run ... head down, count to a hundred, repeat. The miles ticked by, and as I passed the finish line (seeing people finishing, and that's hard, too) and headed out on subsequent laps, I started thinking about what time I might get. If I really belted this, I could go sub-12 hours! I was a little wiser to things now, and I didn't try to smash out the miles, but I did spend a mile or so working out what mile pace I'd have to hit to go sub-12. I worked it out ... and then it didn't work out, because there's always a moment when you flag. First few miles I was running 9 minute miles, but for me that just wasn't sustainable.

It was great to see Andy Holgate there again supporting the race! He was sporting a sling from where he'd had a bike crash on Ironman UK earlier that year, but I stopped for a fist-bump—the undamaged arm of course—and went on my way. He's a great bloke, a passionate advocate for the sport and always supportive and helpful.

Of course, it's partly his fault I was doing ironman racing at all, so at several tough points on the run I wanted to trip him over and kick him into the goose-shit infested lake, broken shoulder or no. He's inspired a lot of people to take up triathlon and enter Ironman races, and as such he's someone who is not only loved and respected, but who is probably the subject of many murderous thoughts from athletes on mile 16 of their Ironman run. Top fella!

I experienced one comedy moment at a feed station—I bit open a gel and squeezed, and succeeded in almost, but not quite, completely missing my mouth. The gel squirted all over my hands, beard and face, much to the amusement of the volunteer there! I giggled along with her and kept running, and for the next two miles I tried licking the end of my nose for a much-needed sugar boost. At the next feed station I poured water over myself so that I could unglue my eyes to see where I was going, and my nostrils so I could breathe.

And oh, those gels.*

(*There's a saying... Never trust a fart in an Ironman. Those gels can mess up your insides if you take too many of them, and some people don't train with them and suffer the unpleasant results. I remember on one middle distance race run, I was running with a woman for a while and we noticed that the guy in front of us had ... well he'd ... hell, there's no easy way to put this. He'd shit himself. I don't know if he knew or not. If he didn't, I didn't want to be the one to tell him and cause embarrassment and distress. If he did know then he was a beast so focussed on his race that he wasn't going to let a small thing like having soiled himself keep him from the finish line. Honestly, I think it was the former, and the other runner and I decided the best tactic was to get past him so we weren't running in his wake. Fug. Whatever. And that poor shitty dude wasn't running that fast.)

Usually I'm fine with gels, because I use them in training and make sure they don't have a nasty effect on my guts. But at Outlaw I spent some time on the run feeling queasy, then feeling the sudden need for a little sit down, if you get my drift. A mate of mine calls those portaloos on an Ironman course Thunder Boxes, but luckily they were close to a feed station blasting rock music to mask any sounds.

Something else I learned that day—if you sit down 11

hours into an Ironman, it can be very, very hard to stand up and start running again.

But get running I did, and through pissing rain I passed the finishing chute on my last 3 mile lap of the lake. For the last painful, hobbly mile down the side of that lake I had a big smile on my face, because I was about to finish my second iron distance race!

And unlike in a branded Ironman, you're allowed to run across the finish line with a member of your family. So I grabbed my son at the start of the finishing chute and we ran over together.

It was glorious, and I'd finished the race in 12 hours 23 minutes. That's still my personal best time, but subsequent races were a bit more ... bumpy. One day I might return to try to get a finishing time with 11 at the beginning ... but maybe not. As I've said before it's the tougher, more gnarly races I really like, but I'll always treasure the memory of becoming an Outlaw. I loved every minute of it. Well, almost. You know what I mean.

We do this because it's fun.

11

WHERE I TRAIN

I'm definitely a country boy at heart. I love the countryside, and my family and I never take where we live for granted. I loved it even before I started getting fit—there were walks in the woods with my kids, and strolls through local lanes with friends to pubs, including that fateful walk on New Year's Day when I was 41 to the Goose & Cuckoo when I thought, *That's it, I'm fat and unfit and too old to turn things around*. That proved to be wrong, and since that moment my love of the countryside and the place where I live has increased exponentially. I even love the smell of muck- spreading, which probably comes from the couple of years we lived on a farm when I was a kid! Ah, the smell of the countryside...

Being outdoors really is beautiful. One of my favourite days during the original Covid lockdown was a walk I went on with my daughter. It was early morning and we wandered down along the Usk Valley Walk, crossing fields until we hit the River Usk, then following the course of the river. We came to a rough bench and sat down for a while, breaking open the flask of coffee and the toast wrapped in foil. The toast was cold, but it didn't matter. The coffee was hot, and good! We'd already seen the usual wildlife common to the area—rabbits, buzzards, and a pair of red kites that have recently started nesting in our local woods. Wonderful birds. As we drank and watched the lazy water drifting by, we saw the glorious luminescent flash of a kingfisher flying upstream. Gorgeous! And just a few moments later we spotted movement on the opposite bank, and it was an otter carrying a huge fish in its mouth! I'm pretty sure that's the only time I've ever seen an otter in the wild. We felt blessed, and walking further along the river I started recounting everything we'd seen.

"...and the kites, then the kingfisher and otter and..." There was a flash of auburn movement ahead of us. "...a fox!" It sauntered out onto the path not thirty feet ahead of us, sniffing the air. We froze, delighted and surprised, and watched as the fox trotted away between the trees.

That's the place where we live. It's paradise, and I love it, and the best thing about this exercise lark is seeing and getting to know so much more of it.

Though the inside-out roadkill I see on a Sunday morning bike ride isn't one of the highlights.

We still walk to local pubs occasionally, but now I'm more likely to stop at a cafe for coffee and a cake whilst on a bike ride on my own or with friends. Honestly, I spend more in coffee shops than pubs nowadays (much to the bemusement of some of my older friends), and long may it continue! And whilst out and about running, biking and wild swimming, I've got to know so much more of Monmouthshire than I ever did before. There are lanes I never knew existed. Hell, there are *villages* I never knew about! One of my favourite bike rides is out from home, up a windy, badly surfaced road to Llantilio Croesenny, then on along the Rockfield road to Monmouth. It's a lovely route, usually very quiet, winding and bumpy and with some gorgeous views and interesting places to pass. One of the houses that's been worked on for years looks like it should be on Grand Designs. And then of course, there's Rockfield studios, the famous recording studio where the likes of Motorhead, Queen, Budgie, The Stone Roses, Oasis, Simple Minds, and many others have stayed and recorded music. I never cycle along that road without thinking of Lemmy heading into Monmouth for a pint of vodka and coke, or Freddie Mercury sat in the back of a Roller being driven to the studio with the opening lyrics of Bohemian Rhapsody going round and round in his mind. I doubt any rock bands head there now wondering which middle-aged blokes in lycra have cycled through those lanes.

It really is beautiful where I live. Spring, summer, autumn, winter, I'm out training in the countryside. Kit choices change, as do routes and training times (I've grown to really dislike when the nights start drawing in, something that didn't really bother me before I started heading out to run, bike or swim in the evenings). But exercise has become such a big part of my life that I try not to let things like darkness, rain, or snow stop me. I know there are more comfortable, warm and smelly ways to train, but I've never been a gym bunny. And though I do have a turbo trainer for my bike—a device which Torquemada himself might have taken a delight in inventing—I'd much rather be out on the roads.

Anyone can do this, wherever you live. I'm very lucky here, but even if you live in a city there are run and bike routes that might surprise you. Get out and look around. Ask locals. Look at an OS map and check out some local footpaths. Or just get the hell out on two wheels or two feet and get lost for a while, and I guarantee you'll be surprised at the places you find, some of which you might have never known were there.

I've learned a lot training around here, about my own training methods and thresholds, what I like and what I don't, and how living in a place where there are hills wherever I go in any direction is a huge positive! I've lost count of the number of races I've done where, mingling around afterwards or grabbing food and coffee while the sweat still dries on your kit, I hear fellow competitors talking about the 'terrible hills' and I find myself thinking, *What? There were hills?* It's a big advantage living and training in a place where the hills are always out to get you.

Swimming

Until I entered my first Ironman I could barely swim front crawl at all. I learned quickly once I'd joined the NEWTs. and the most enjoyable aspect of the club for me quickly became the outdoor swimming. This was something I'd never done before––I mean, who the hell wants to jump in a dirty river or lake?––but after swimming in a pool twice a week dodging drifting wads of hair or plasters and opaque patches of spittle, a lake seemed like a really good idea.

My first time in a wetsuit felt like I was being crushed from all angles at the same time by a giant gorilla who'd been doing specific 'crushing humans' exercises. I was assured that this was fine, this was normal, and I nodded my understanding because I couldn't speak, and I was more concerned with the idea that I'd soon be immersed in cold lake water unable to breathe. And my first time in a lake with the NEWTs was pretty bloody terrifying. We swam in a reservoir supplying the golf course at the Celtic Manor

Resort (one of our coaches worked there and we had special permission to do so, though swimming is otherwise strictly prohibited), and my first few times in the water caused quite a few panicky moments. *The wetsuit is too tight, I can't breathe! The water's murky what's down there? It's too cold!*

But I soon grew to love it. And I also learned that I was pretty okay in the cold. There's that first few moments when you get in and hyperventilate, but that's natural and not something to panic about. It's your body adjusting to keep you warm. Then there's the bit where you first dunk your head under the cold water. Remember ice cream head? Nasty. But that, too, becomes easier, and a vital part of acclimatising your body ready for the open water swim. I'm okay with the cold, and it could be that compared to some of the true racing snakes we have in the club, I have a little more 'padding' (ref: my love of cake).

As well as the Celtic Manor reservoir I've swam in the sea at several locations, and also for a few weeks in 2020 when there was a brief summer respite in the Covid lockdown in our area, the lovely Llandegford Reservoir. But my favourite place to swim is the River Usk. There's a route starting from Usk town that leads up to an area of rapids and back down again. It clocks in at a mile up and down, and I've never swum that length of river the same way twice. As well as changing from year to year with tree-falls and the river bed moving, it also changes week on week, when water level will dictate the rate of flow, and weeds etc will alter throughout the year. It's become quite a social pace to swim and train, and there are often a group of people sitting around the rapids in wetsuits (and some without!) chatting before jumping in for a rapid return to Usk.

And that's one of the great aspects of river swimming—swim against the current and it's a tough workout, and indeed sometimes it feels like you're battling to move forward and the bank is moving so slowly and *am I actually just a shit swimmer?* But jump back in from the rapids and power back down with the current, and for just a little while you feel like a *real* swimmer, watching the river bed rushing by at a rate of knots. Lovely fun.

I've met fellow triathletes who are superb in the pool but who go to pieces in open water. Maybe it's the mass starts (I've grown to quite enjoy the bump and bash of hundreds of swimmers all starting at the same time and aiming at the same place), or sometimes it's a fear of open water. Sometimes in a race you can barely see your hand in front of your face, and this can be disconcerting. But train outdoors as much as you can when the water's warm enough, and when you race you'll be ready.

Pool training is great for endurance, specific swim sets, technique, and everything else. But open water swimming is where you learn to race.

Biking

I live in one of the best areas in Britain for cycling. People come here from elsewhere to ride their bikes, and I live right in the middle of it all! It's the sweet-toothed version of actually living *in* a cake shop. There are hills everywhere, and countless routes from my house to suit any time or distance I want to ride. There are also some bloody splendid cafes, and I have frequented many of them. I ride around 2,000 miles each year around Monmouthshire, occasionally into Newport county, and sometimes up into Powys, and I never tire of it. I stick mainly to quieter roads and know the busy roads to avoid––I hate having queues of traffic behind me, it's not fair to the drivers, and over the years I've come to learn that if you're considerate to drivers, they'll return that treatment. However hard you're training, it won't affect your finishing time in a forthcoming race if you drift into a gate opening to let a few cars pass you on a winding road. And it's actually quite satisfying receiving a toot of thanks from a driver.

And here I go digressing again, but it's an important aside to talk about cycling safety and other road users. There's this constant tension between some cyclists, and some drivers. I often hear drivers talk about 'bloody cyclists', and the same goes the other way. It's a minority either way, but as usual in these cases the minority makes more noise and causes problems for all. Over the past ten years I've probably cycled 20,000 miles, and other than racing distance, the vast majority of those miles have been in and around Monmouthshire. In that time I've fallen off my bike maybe 4 times. Three times were almost static, when I failed to unclip my shoes from the pedals fast enough, or on the wrong side. Yes, hysterical, I can almost hear you laughing, but it will happen to you too. The other time I took a fall was when I hit a pothole on my TT bike and met the ground at around 25mph. That resulted in a cracked rib, some blood, and a guffaw of laughter from Tracey when I finally made it home. She was full of pity.

I've had no major incidents involving drivers. Sure, quite a few near misses, some of which resulted in me shouting and gesticulating and probably only ever being seen by other people, not the driver I'm aiming said shouts and gesticulations at. A variety of bad driving causes these near misses:

Drivers who don't like crossing the white line when overtaking a cyclist, resulting in a close elbow-shave from a wing mirror. Sometimes I'll even feel the breeze of a car whizzing past at fifty. That's not a nice experience.

Drivers who can't wait to overtake on a narrow country road.

Drivers who don't realise how fast you might be travelling towards them and pull out of a junction in front of you.

Usually, safe cycling, and being aware of what's going on around you, can prevent many of these instances from happening. Cycle as you drive—ears and eyes open, looking for potential hazards, and always assuming that problems will come from other peoples' driving, not your cycling.

If you're a considerate cyclist (or driver), problems will usually pass you by. But I always remember that between me and a nasty road rash there's just a thin layer of lycra. I'm always as considerate of other road users as I can be, especially on the quiet country roads I usually stick to. I'd rather slow down and wave a car past than ride with a vehicle itching to overtake me. It's better for my nerves. And better for my limbs, skin, bones and bike if I don't end up in the hedge.

All that said, there's no cure for being an arsehole. And I have encountered a few during ten years of wheeling along the local roads. The most memorable incident involved me and two friends out for a long Saturday ride. We were bimbling along a very long, wide, safe road, and a couple of us were two abreast. Like a half-rusted cliche from hell, a white van roared past us with horn blaring and the angry-faced overweight driver shouting words from the open passenger window which involved various nicknames for male and female sexual organs, mixed up in, I must admit, a startlingly creative and memorable manner. The driver revved, slowed, revved again, driving alongside us in a very aggressive and threatening way. He was trying to make his van's abused engine say, *You lookin'? You want some?* I think nowadays the agitated gentleman would be called a 'gammon'. I was suitably perturbed, even more so when one of my friends attempted to calm and soothe the furious driver by shouting, "Read the Highway Code, wanker!" This drove him into a greater frenzy. If we'd responded with a similar tirade of genitalia-associated language, perhaps he wouldn't have been so incensed. He might even have been impressed at our creativity in his chosen field of conversation. But no. He wanted a fight. He accelerated ahead to a lay-by and pulled in, and I thought to myself, *This is when the back doors open and seven more pink-faced angry men jump out and start shouting more inside-your-underwear inspired words our way in preparation of pulling us off our bikes and taking it in turns to stand on our heads.*

Luckily there was just the driver, posturing beside his vehicle with bare belly spilling out over his greasy jeans and rosy-red face struggling to suck in enough air to keep calling us penises. We rode past with a smile and a wave––that was a good high-intensity quarter of a mile sprint session––and a minute later he overtook us again, revving the motor in his large and heavy metal vehicle at three cyclists in a very brave manner, and he disappeared in a haze of rage and high blood pressure.

So be as careful as you can, never pour fuel on a flammable situation, and always remember that sometimes, people are just arseholes. They're born arseholes, they spend their lives being arseholes, and I'll give you two guesses how they die.

That was just one time in 20,000 miles, so fear not. It's like when it's fine swimming in the Med, even though there are white sharks there. *Usually* you'll be okay.

I've never let experiences like that spoil my enjoyment of

cycling. It's truly one of my favourite things to do, and I've discovered some really beautiful routes around areas I'd have never visited before. In some of these remote locations, I do sometimes worry a little about having a mechanical. If I had an issue I couldn't fix at the roadside (I'm not very mechanically minded, and can just about change a tube) and had to call my wife for rescue, having to describe to her where I was might be a big problem! Here's a tip––download the app 'what3words'. It allocates three random words to *every square 3 metres on the planet*! That's pretty stunning, and you can pinpoint your location to anyone in the world at any time.

For instance, I lost my virginity outside a disco thirty-five years ago at streaking.seducing.flocking (honest). I finished my first Ironman round about puns.villa.necks. And the angry driver wanted to fight us at linguists.zealous.grills.

It's difficult to go for a ride anywhere here and not hit any hills. One of my favourite quick rides is a 20 miler from my house to Usk, Raglan, and back again, and even that route has a couple of options from Usk to Raglan––flat and fast, or hilly and tough. There's the Tumble close by, a major climb up to the top of the Blorenge mountain, and this is a climb known nationally. There's a hill called the Dark Side, a climb up to Wentwood Forest whose name pretty much says it all. There are other great hills, but it's the quieter country lanes I most enjoy. My knowledge of the area I love has improved hugely since I've been riding, but even so I still occasionally come across places I don't know.

And there are great cafes in Usk, Abergavenny, Crickhowell, Tintern, Monmouth ... you can see I've done my research. Cake in the name of fitness.

I'm going to get that on a tee shirt.

Running

I go running morning, noon or night, any season of the year, any day of the week. I've grown to prefer trail running, but there are some great road routes around me too, mainly on the quieter lanes. Trail runs can be relatively flat, following the course of the river Usk or the Monmouthshire & Brecon canal, or very hilly, heading up into the hills above where I live towards the trig point, folly tower, and the remote memorial to the crew of a Blenheim bomber that crashed up there during WW2.

One of my favourite quick runs is just four miles long, but from door to door it takes in four small woodlands and a stretch along a beautiful canal towpath, with less than a mile of road.

I'll go out in blazing sunlight with a water bottle and hit the roads, clocking up ten miles and hardly seeing any traffic. Or I'll run in the winter after dark, sporting a head torch, following the canal towpath or the trails, seeing different coloured eyes reflecting my torchlight back at me as creatures stare in wonder, or maybe hunger, at this strange human invading their night.

There's a great 5k road route door to door, a loop my family discovered during lockdown for Covid and which is now a semi-regular test of speed and fitness. I used to be edging towards 20 minutes for a 5k, now I'm up around 24 minutes again, but now I know about that 5k route it's always there if time is tight or I only fancy a short, sharp run.

Sometimes I'll go farther afield, jumping in the car and driving to one of the local mountains around Abergavenny. On the Blorenge there's a great 7 mile loop along trails up, down and around the mountain, most of it on establish trails but with some really tough climbs. For a while I was doing this run every Friday morning, and often I'd complete the 7 miles without seeing another soul, change in the car park, then head into town for breakfast at one of the great Abergavenny cafes. I like the Skirrid too, and that's a favourite night run for me, involving a hard, steep initial climb, then a run along the long ridge to the trig point. The nighttime views from up there are fantastic.

I'll also sometimes multi-task. If my son's playing rugby in Abergavenny I'll go to watch (I do my utmost not to miss a match if at all possible) and then run home along the canal, a nice, and often muddy, 8 miles.

Running's the exercise you can do almost anywhere and with minimal kit. If I go away to a writing convention I'll often take my running kit with me, and it's a great way to explore an unknown city or area. I've run in Glasgow, Birmingham, Derby, Bristol, New York, and Los Angeles, among many other places I can't even remember. Great fun.

In my early forties I mainly ran on the roads, because I didn't really know anything else. I'd be targetting 5k or 10k races, before moving up to longer distances, and for a while it was all about the time. But living where I do, it was inevitable that I'd hit the trails, and really I've never looked back. I do still run on the roads now, and sometimes it's quite a nice change picking up some speed and finding those old lanes again. But my love is fields and mud, hills and solitude. Trail running is terrific training too, whatever your target race. You'll inevitably find some hills, great for power and anaerobic training, and if you're a real glutton for punishment you can find a muddy hill for some repeats. You can also find flat zones for some interval training. And every trail run is a Fartlek session! When I was first training in my early forties, I'd worry if I was doing too much trail running as I wasn't fitting in the right sessions from my plan. But I firmly believe that juggling short and longer trail sessions will give you the training load you need. Unless, as I've said before, you're at the pointy end of the field and looking to podium.

Trail running is also kinder on your joints (just watch your footing), and with each footfall being slightly different it's great for building muscles and flexibility around your ankles and calves. Great for balance, too. And if you're caught short, it's much easier and more socially acceptable taking a leak on a sheltered hillside trail than it is on the pavement outside Greggs.

I'm totally spoiled for choice where I live, and there are still trails and paths I've never tried, I'm sure. But my favourite run is still the Blorenge mountain, early in the morning, with just the sheep and the birds and the gently rising mist keeping me company. It's food for the soul.

12

EGO, OR, 'YOU'VE RUN A MARATHON? HOW CUTE.'

I 've recently got into a band called Idles, a punk outfit with a real social conscience and a contagious energy and passion to their performances. I watched an interview with their lead singer just after they'd come off stage after their extraordinary 2019 Glastonbury appearance, and behind his usual deadpan expression you could tell he was buzzing. And he said something that really struck a chord with me (and I paraphrase): "Sometimes it's perfectly valid to pat yourselves on the back for a job well done."

Finishing a race isn't gigging at Glastonbury, but it is still an achievement, and it's worth celebrating. It's worth feeling good about yourself. Ego? Yeah. A little.

It's sometimes delicate to talk about, because most people don't like to be seen to be showing off. But it's definitely part of anyone's fitness journey to be able to feel good about what they're doing. I started my 5th decade on this planet overweight and unfit, and finished it a changed person, physically and mentally. I'm able to tackle things now that I wouldn't have attempted a decade ago, and not

just physical things. Training for, and finishing my first
Ironman changed my life, gave me a huge amount of self-
belief, boosted my confidence, and that quote I love so
much—

If you think you can do something, or think you can't, you're
probably right

——has given me much more of a can-do attitude.

I remember moments after finishing Ironman UK,
Tracey and my kids were there, as was Andy Holgate, and
we were milling around and I was desperate to take out my
contact lenses. I asked Tracey if she had a make-up mirror
in her bag I could use to do this, and she said, "Get a bloody
grip. You've just done an Ironman." Ha! She was right. I took
out those lenses. A stupid, tiny example, but it's also rele-
vant. It's developing a can-do attitude. If you can do an ironman, you can do anything.

Most races I take part in start at stupid-o'clock on a
Sunday morning, and swimming away from the start at 6
a.m. in a freezing lake with hundreds of like-minded people
around me, virtually every time I think of the majority of
people I know still lying in bed, some of them with a hang-
over. I've often finished a race by the time most people I
know are getting up. And I like that. I like driving home
from a distant race and seeing the ghostly glow of TVs from
behind drawn curtains, and wondering how many other
people have done something today that makes them feel
good, makes them feel strong, makes them feel even a little
bit proud.

Another good quote:

Pain is temporary. Bragging rights last a lifetime.

I'm not sure if it's a quote particular to Ironman or more general, but it's certainly something that most athletes I know do to a greater or lesser extent (and I use the term athlete here to cover sub-9 hour ironman racers, and those who train for 5k races).

You can't talk about ego without exposing it, and being falsely humble is sometimes even more annoying than just being up-front with it. It doesn't have to sound big-headed when it's a statement of fact! I've done 5 ironman races, a dozen halfs, and I've lost count of the number of other triathlons, running and biking races I've completed over the past ten years, and I love talking about what I've done. That's part of the reason for writing this book—talking about what I've achieved because it's fun to look back, and also in the hope that it might inspire other people to take on their own challenge, and perhaps even change their own lives.

Yes, I'm proud of what I've done. I like being fitter than I've ever been before. Triathlon club members aside, I'm probably as fit as, or fitter than most people of my age I know. I enjoy talking about what I do. I like the words of respectful praise as much as the 'you must be fucking mad' comments (that usually come from people who don't exercise and can't understand the allure or benefits of doing so).

Okay, that's quite enough of that. But ... uncomfortable though it is to expose your own ego like this, I hope it makes anyone reading aware that it's not necessarily a bad thing. Deciding to improve your life by getting fitter, faster, stronger, or whatever, especially at an age where some people might think it's too late (I did), is deserving of a certain amount of satisfaction. It's not a sin. It's natural, and so long as you don't let it run away with you, I believe it's healthy too. It helps to drive you further and push harder.

The Idles singer was right ... sometimes it's OK to pat yourself on the back (but beware of shoulder injuries).

13

RACE REPORT:

IRONMAN WALES—18TH SEPTEMBER, 2016

Whatever I first thought about doing an Ironman my immediate first choice was Ironman Wales, but the sea swim put me off. At the time I could barely swim, and the thought of a potentially choppy sea swim, with jellyfish chasing me, was a bit too much. That's why IMUK was my first—lake swim, no jellyfish. I bailed on IM Wales 2014 because of a knee injury, then I raced Outlaw in 2015.

So it turned out that 2016 was my year to face the dragon. It was heartbreaking. It was horrible. It was epic. As with the other race reports, the account below was written at the time, tweaked only so that it fits well into this book.

Do you hear that? Thun-der... da na na na, na na na, na!

IRONMAN WALES

TENBY IS my new favourite town. I mean it. I've never experienced anything like Ironman Wales. What an epic day, filled with pain and cheering, sweat and hollering, aching legs and 'high-five-for-power' boards, a few dark moments and countless moment of delight. And Tenby was the shouting, cheering, beating heart of it all.

My wife and kids came down with me for the weekend. We arrived later Friday night, so Saturday was a bit frazzled—registration, briefing, checking and bagging my kit, racking bike and bags, then watching my son smash Ironkids. After that we chilled for a bit, with a nice meal in our flat and a glass of wine to try and ease me to sleep. And ... by some miracle I did sleep! Only 3 or 4 hours, perhaps, but that 4:30 alarm call didn't fill me with despair. In fact, I was excited! This being my third iron-distance race helped, but also the idea of racing one of the most epic, famous, and perhaps one of the toughest Ironman courses in the world filled me with nervous energy. I was one of 18 members of the NEWTs racing, so I knew there was going to be a massive support contingent there too. When you're seeing red, there's nothing like a sea of yellow and black to encourage you on.

I ate breakfast (the trusty porridge with banana and honey ... if I ever went off-piste on race morning I think I'd explode) and got ready, then bid my family farewell and walked down to transition on my own. I felt good. There were some troubled faces around, but though I had a few butterflies, I couldn't wait to hit the beach and get going. The atmosphere in transition was electric, and I saw a few mates. I was already getting the feeling that this was going to be a fantastic day.

The walk down to the beach was great fun. The early morning streets were thronged with people, and I saw a few NEWT mates already cheering us on. I mean, we were all easy to see... I was the one in the black wetsuit and white swim hat.

Once we were hanging our shoe bags for the run back up from the beach to T1 (there's a 1km run up steep steps and through the Tenby streets, all classed as part of the first transition), the whole 'self-seeding' thing went in the bin, and I found myself down on the beach pretty near the front. I'd placed myself in the 1:20 pen, but was hoping for quicker, so I wasn't too troubled. Saw some more NEWT friends on the paths and steps above the beach, some of them flying the classic 'don't be shit' Welsh flag that has become quite well known!

What a wait that was. A beautiful sunrise bled across the horizon. Thousands of people lined the cliffs, steps, ramps and the roads above, and somewhere in there I knew would be Tracey, Ellie and Dan. And when the Welsh national anthem began, what a spine-tingling moment that was. Got a speck of sand in my eye, I reckon.

Then AC/DC's *Thunderstruck* blasted the speck away, and we were off.

Those first couple of hundred metres swimming were fine, not too much bumping and punching because of the rolling start, and soon I fell into a decent rhythm. The first buoy, however, was a real rumble, with scores of swimmers trying to get around at the same time. A few bumps and kicks here, and then I was pushed against and down the side of the huge buoy, and forced underneath. That was my first mouthful of sea water. Admission: I'd not done much sea training, so that sea water was burning my throat and making me gag. Especially when it was supplemented with a nice dose of fuel from the boats and jet-skis. Euch! Note to self: train for the swim properly next time, numpty!

Lap one done, and I was feeling good. I'm always more comfortable on lap two, but by the first buoy I was keen to get it over with. And then ... The Jellyfish. Anyone who saw that Leviathan at the first buoy on lap 2 will know what I'm on about. Sure, I'd seen a few before. But compared to this, they were like sparrows sitting beside a buzzard. It was a bloody monster. You've seen *Jurassic Park*, right? Or *The Blob*? This was bigger. More stings. And I punched that bastard in the head. Or maybe it was in the arse. You just can't tell with a jellyfish.

Could be a contributory factor to my 1:10 pb swim!

I was a bit wobbly up the ramps, then I found my feet and started the run into town. And this was when I began to realise just what the legendary Ironman Wales support is all about. There were thousands of people lining those early morning streets, cheering and screaming, and I ran the 1k from beach to transition grinning like a hyena in a Beefeater, especially when I saw my lovely wife and kids cheering me on.

T1 went smoothly, then I was out on the bike course. This was the bit I was nervous about. It's a legendary ride, with 8,000 feet of climbing over the 112 miles, and although I'd ridden the course three years before during Long Course Weekend, I hadn't been there since. But I needn't have worried. I settled into the ride quite comfortably, taking on some food and drink and an occasional Saltstick tab to prevent cramping.

Then on a narrow lane out towards Angle a motorbike marshal gave me a blue card for overtaking in a supposed no overtaking zone. What the hell! I tried to process what had happened. And there'll be more about this later...

I worried about the penalty for a while, and vowed that I'd be extra careful with the rest of my race. Didn't want to pick up more penalties and get DQ'd! I saw plenty of drafting, and sometimes it was just impossible to leave the required distances. But I was cautious––no peeing in public, observing drafting zones as much as I could, and the bike went well. The hills were fun, and I realised how all that hilly training was paying off. While I'm not exactly Brad Wiggins on the flat, I often overtook people going uphill. Some people were even pushing up Wiseman's Bridge the first time, but though I found the route challenging, it was also beautiful.

And the support was utterly immense. The towns and villages were thronged with people, all up early and lining the streets and sitting outside houses, firing up barbecues and drinking some very tempting cups of tea. I saw the results of a few nasty crashes, a few mechanicals, but overall the race was pretty smooth. Then I passed Tenby and Kiln Park, and there was NEWT Hill. One of the guys (Gareth) was on megaphone duty, and I heard him shouting, "And here's Tim Lebbon!" I had a smile on my face from that moment, and my daughter's video of me going up that hill shows a gurning idiot swerving all over the road as he pumps his fist. Yep, that was me.

If you're a NEWT, that place provides an injection of pure power that launches you on the next 20 miles. If you're not a NEWT, you're still cheered and hollered up that hill by up to a hundred supporters sporting the yellow and black colours. It was amazing, and seeing my club-mates and family gave me a massive, massive boost.

The second lap, and that final 40 miles, was tougher. Some bastard had obviously gone around and made the hills steeper. At the top of Wiseman's the second time I met Jon, the guy I'd met on that horrible steep hill in the Titan triathlon a couple of months before. Hill buddies yet again! I finally rolled into Tenby and T2, and went to the penalty tent and served my 5 minute penalty. While I was there with the penalty guy the Race Ref turned up, and the three of us chatted about what a tough job they have. They said how unpleasant it is if they actually have to DQ people.

Hmmm.

This is the part of the race where I usually think, "Almost finished!" Yeah, just the matter of an ironman run (marathon) to contend with. But it was great to get off the bike, and that first little jog through Tenby was a noisy, rowdy delight. Cheeks aching from smiling, smiling to set aside my painful feet, I made the first hilly lap out to New Hedges and back into town. I saw Mark, an old friend I'd bumped into the day before who I hadn't seen for almost twenty years, and that was nice. Then running around one of the quieter backstreets bits of Tenby (and there aren't many of them), my family were waiting outside our apartment. Our friends the Coopers were there too, they'd come down for the day to support––good mates, eh? That was a great moment.

I saw Mark again once or twice through Tenby, he must have been one of the fastest runners there that day, darting back and forth through town to catch me two or three times per lap!

(Current note: Mark and I have since caught up a lot more ... he found that day so inspirational that he joined the NEWTs, trained hard, and it was my honour to return the favour and watch him race in Tenby the following year. Top bloke).

Lap two of the run was harder. Loads more support, some getting steadily more drunk in town, and I made a cheeky diversion towards the finisher's chute (if only!) before veering away again. Saw my family and the Coopers again, and loads of NEWTS, and a few other mates in the crowd.

Everyone has a dark time during an Ironman. Mine was lap 3 of the run. I was hurting, my legs were weak, and however much I drank I felt dehydrated, water swilling around in my stomach and making me feel queasy. Seeing some friends on the run helped—some of the other NEWTs racing, Jeff Johnson from the USA, my hill-buddy Jon, and others. But though I was in a dark moment, I never once considered not finishing.

I saw everyone again back through Tenby, and the town was alight now, darkness had fallen and the whole place was illuminated. It was ablaze with a staggering amount of support, on fire with good cheer, and as I completed my last lap this was it, this was me heading back down into town and towards the finish line. That was a real moment. The crowd cheered, I heard that wonderful, "Tim, you are an Ironman!" and then I saw my wife and kids right next to the finish. I gave my wife a hug and kiss and the moment I stopped my legs went. Desperate not to resort to 'the crawl', I shoved myself from the hoardings and crossed the line. Arms up. Cheeks hurting from smiling.

Ironman Wales, done. Swim 1:10, bike 7:15, run a tough 4:50. With transitions (and 5 minute penalty) a total of 13:45. I'm no racing snake, but my target had been 14 hours, so I was a very happy man. And yes, of course, I'm already thinking how I could probably go sub-13 if I work hard to improve my run...

Back at our apartment on one of the quieter streets, we cheered on the runners from the balcony, and I even managed a curry and a couple of beers. I was high as a kite and exhausted, aching and sore, and I felt bloody wonderful.

(A brief aside, and back to that penalty card I received earlier and which I'd like to talk about some more. There's a *lot* I could write about this, but I'd rather keep it short so as not to detract from the joy of the day. So, on the Monday I discovered I'd been disqualified. Turns out they didn't record me taking my penalty, so they DQ'd me for that. It also turns out I should have *never* been given that penalty anyway—there was no official no-passing zone, the sign that the referee saw was from another race—so it was a double error on their part. It took ten long, horrible, angst-filled days—days when my wife and I had taken the week off work and were supposed to be chilling and basking in celebratory delight—to clear my DQ, and I now have my time reinstated. I'm so glad they scrapped the DQ, but it really wasn't a very pleasant few days).

But enough of that. This was my third Ironman, but *definitely* the best. The support in Tenby is beyond description ... you really have to experience it to understand. It was one of my best days ever, made even more epic by the friends and supporters who went down to cheer us on. A special shout-out to my old mate Mark (who seemed to be everywhere in Tenby!), my friends the Coopers, all the NEWTS and other guys I know from triathlon who screamed my name just when I needed it, and especially to my lovely wife and kids. They were on the beach at 6:30am, at the finish line at 9pm, and at every point in between, and at the end of the race they kept complaining about how tired they were. They're wonderful.

14

THE INEVITABLE CAKE

Earlier I jokingly said I'd devote an entire chapter to cake. Ridiculous, right?

Well...

I have a very sweet tooth. It's something I'm trying to control, because I know it's not really good for me. But it's always been the case, and getting into exercise, and becoming fitter in my forties, has only exacerbated the problem. Or rather, situation. I try not to look on it as a problem.

Flapjacks, Victoria sponge, salted caramel muffins, cheesecake of all shapes and colours and flavours, Battenburg (fight me), chocolate cake, lemon tarts, bakewell tarts, fairy cakes (fight me again), mince pies ... the list is long. The struggle is real.

It doesn't help when I mention my addiction to people and they say, 'Well it's fine, you burn it all off'. I look at my waistline and realise it's really not fine. Sure, I train a lot, but I also eat a lot. I went vegetarian a little over a year ago, and it feels good and I don't miss meat at all, but I'm the same weight and shape as before I began. If anything, after lockdown in 2020 because of Covid, I'm a little rounder and softer (curiously I haven't put on any weight during lock-down, but I'm definitely become a little more 'comfortable'). So even though when I'm told I 'burn it all off' I rationalise it and tend to agree, subconsciously I know that's really not the case. Eating crap is eating crap, however much exercise you do. It might be the case that it doesn't mean you pile on the pounds, but you're still putting that crap into your body.

Diet is a really important part of training. During my first couple of years of getting fit, when I'd committed to racing my first Ironman, I considered dropping the booze for a year and eating as clean as I could. The booze lasted for a month (dry January), and the clean eating didn't really begin. I've always toyed with dieting, and though I don't think I've ever been *massively* overweight, it's often been on my mind. But we all know that dieting to lose weight doesn't work. Cut down all you want, lose a few pounds quickly and your body goes into famine mode, and soon you're shovel-ling food down your gullet again. What dieting *does* do is pile billions of pounds into the bank accounts of people who push fads.

Eat less, and better. Exercise more. You can have that diet plan for free.

That's been one great thing about me starting to get fit, and continuing with exercise, training and racing all through my forties, and now into my fifties (and how the *hell* did I get that old without noticing?). Even when I occasion-ally hit a flat period when I might go a few weeks with low mojo, and training becomes pretty staggered, I don't tend to put on weight. I genuinely believe that what I've done has changed my physiology (and not only the added creases on my face from a bit of weight loss and much less of a butt, as my wife often points out). My comfortable weight is now around 172 pounds, and my racing weight—zeroing in on an

Ironman, and if I've been training well—is maybe ten pounds lighter than that. Interestingly, a BMI index will tell me that 172 pounds is overweight for my height, and maybe now, yeah, slightly. But I have issues with the whole BMI thing because there's so much it doesn't take into account. It tells me that a healthy weight range for me begins at over thirty pounds lighter than I am! Did you see Christian Bale in that movie *The Machinist*?

However, I am eating better now than I ever have before. Breakfast is either porridge or granola, loaded with nuts and seeds and dried fruit, blueberries, banana, a tablespoon of milled flaxseed, and sometimes a drizzle of honey. That's been my standard brekkie for some time, making sure I get a good hit of fruit inside me in case I don't eat any for the rest of the day. I try to get my veg intake too, and especially since going vegetarian, that's working more and more. Cheese on toast for lunch, though ... I try to keep that to once or twice a week.

But I still balance out the good stuff with too much bad stuff. Because there's still the cake.

Here's one of my very favourite things to do: go for a longish bike ride, on my own or preferably in company with friends from the tri club or elsewhere, and stopping somewhere for a coffee and a cake (as an aside in this cake chapter, I do also have something of an addiction to coffee. Only a couple of cups per day, but if I don't have one I'm climbing the walls. And coffee and cake go together like strawberries and cream ... toast and jam ... Morecambe and Wise). It's fuel. It's delightfuel. And with the mates I ride with, it is almost inevitafuel.

I don't worry about it too much, though. Because you've got to live. And when it comes to exercise and racing, as I've said a few times already in this account, and as I tell myself at some point during every single race I take part in ... I'm doing this for fun. Fitness is a side benefit of enjoying running and biking and swimming, and cake is a side benefit of being fitter! There. I've rationalised it away yet again.

So it's good to find the right balance. And to finish this chapter I'd like to talk about Star Wars. No, not Jabba The Hutt versus a skinny C3Po. But the Force. In the movies we're all familiar with there's the dark side and the light side, bad and good, and while there are those who struggle between the two, they're still pretty polarised concepts. You wouldn't imagine Darth Maul sitting down for a discussion on the dangerous deforestation of Endor with a family of Ewoks. Neither can you imagine Luke dropping a cheeky Wookie turd into someone's ale in Mos Eisley spaceport.

There's no shades of grey. It's all dark or light.

Except in the Star Wars novel I wrote, *Into the Void*. This was set 25,000 years before the original trilogy, in an era known as the Dawn of the Jedi, and in that time people would strive to live with the Force in balance, not swaying too much one way or the other. It made for a healthier outlook, less angsty star-gazing, and not so many lightsaber decapitations.

And so it is with cake. And here, I'll use cake as a general catch-all metaphor for food and drink you might enjoy, even though you know it's not necessarily that good for you. Cake with a lovely cappuccino is the dark side, undrizzled salad leaves the light. Accept that you can enjoy both, and live in balance, and that'll make you a much happier athlete.

As the great Yoda himself might say, 'What you fancy, does you good, a little bit of always.'

15

EXERCISE IS MENTAL

Exercise is therapy. I'm no doctor or expert on the matter, but any doctor or expert will tell you that a daily dose of nature is good for you, and exercise—indoors in a sweaty gym if you absolutely have to, outside in nature with green around you and blue above, if you can—boosts mental health. There's science to it, and chemicals, but I say this from pure experience.

I'm pretty lucky when it comes to mental health. I have low periods, as everyone does, but I've never been on medication, and have never suffered from depression or intense anxiety. I do wonder, though, what the Tim of now would look and be like if I hadn't taken on the Three Peaks Challenge when I was 41. If I'd stared into that pint glass on New Year's Day and found it empty in more than just the literal sense, and had actually accepted that it was too late to do anything about my fitness, I wonder what I'd be like now?

I don't want to think about it. But I do, because one of my faults (so I'm told, and I dwell on this an awful lot for days on end and tend to agree most of the time) is that I overthink things. I'm not sure whether I overthink things because I'm a writer, or if I'm a writer because I overthink things. I'll have to have a think about that. I do think if I hadn't made a big and quite sudden life change a decade ago, I'd be more overweight now, probably unable to climb our local mountains, let along run up and down them, and without a doubt I'd be less happy. Even when I go through occasional times when my mojo is low and my training haphazard, I still can't imagine *not* living like I do now. Really, it doesn't bear thinking about.

And that's because there's no downside to getting fit.

(An aside here: throughout this meandering and some-what waffling account of my last decade, I've used the term 'got fit' a few times, and every time I write it down I cringe a little. Maybe I should flip back and read what I wrote about Ego, but the humble me winces when I say 'I got fit'. That's because saying that is indirectly comparing myself to other people ... those I know who are my age and who are winning triathlons and qualifying for Kona, and who when I set myself against I'm most certainly nowhere close to their level of fitness. But I'm much fitter now than I would have been if I hadn't spent the last ten years doing all the exercise I love. That's obvious. So I'll just get used to using the word 'fit' as applied to me and understanding that it's not a catch-all term and is on a sliding scale, instead of juggling with 'comparatively fit', or 'got a little bit fitter', or 'got the stage where I could run 10k any day of the week'. And I hope you're OK with that and it doesn't sound pompous. But then, this book is subtitled 'How I Got Fit In My Forties', which sounds much better than 'How I Got A Little Bit Fitter Than I Was But Not Quite As Fit As Some Of The People I Know, In My Forties'. See? I don't overthink things at all.)

It's true. There's no downside to being fit, there's no downside to deciding to get fit, and I honestly believe there's absolutely no time limit on when you can make this choice. I've seen evidence of that around my village during the Covid pandemic and lockdowns, with people I've hardly ever seen out before donning shorts and running top and starting to amble, then jog, then run. It's great to see.

I've had so many people telling me I'm mad for doing what I do. Quite often, these people are overweight and unfit. That's probably not a politically correct comment or observation, but it's true. So who's the mad one?

Exercise boosts your mental wellbeing in so many ways, both physiological and psychological, that I think you're mad if you *don't* do it. Yes, it's hard to begin with, but the benefits are there right at the beginning! I was going to write, 'the benefits outweigh the downsides ...'

... but there are no downsides!

Do I sound preachy? I've heard it said that the only person more annoying than a lifelong non-smoker is one who's stopped smoking. Well, I haven't always been fit, but I changed and got there eventually.

So bollocks to it, I'm going to preach. Here, then, are the ways that taking exercise and being fit––whatever 'fit' means for you, and it's a completely subjective take for anyone–– can benefit you. And yes, some of these are physical bene-fits, some psychological ... but it's all mental. Physical improvements in your body and fitness can only boost your mental wellbeing.

Bear in mind (yet again) that I'm no expert, but this is how exercising and becoming fit has helped me:

Seeing more of nature––rarely a day goes by when I don't spend some time outside. Less so in the winter, perhaps, but I still walk and run, and bike if I can get out during the day.

It's great discovering more of where you live, and I like nothing more than exploring lanes I haven't run or cycled before and seeing where they go and emerge. Sometimes I'm even lucky enough to find a cafe I haven't visited before! I've always been a nature lover (as a kid I was member of the YOC––Young Ornithologists's Club, anyone remember them?), and I'll often stop when I'm out to watch a red kite circling up above, or a fox scampering through remote woodland. Lovely. Now that I've stopped eating animals, I even see cattle in a new light. Seeing more of nature, connecting with it in ways you might not if you're not exercising in it every day, makes you feel more part of nature as well. That's good for you, and it's good for the planet, too.

Me-time––there's a certain selfishness to training for endurance racing ... but being fit and healthy for your family I think balances that out. What it does mean is that you have plenty of time to yourself running, swimming and cycling. And most of the time I think this is pretty healthy. Life is busy, and though biking 70 miles on a Saturday morning isn't relaxing, it is switching off from everything else. You can focus on yourself, the ride, the road. Sometimes you can think things through. Other times it's just a case of the exercise blowing away cobwebs and leaving you ready to enter back into 'normal' life again when you get home. Not everyone likes solitude or is comfortable in their own company, but I like those hours on my own. And if you train with other people you can be as flexible as you like, or need to be, with those long solo hours when it's just you and the road or trails.

Feeling wonderfully knackered––there's nothing quite like the feeling of being tired and worn out after a good workout or race. It's an energised tiredness, the powerful and legal buzz of an endorphin rush. There's probably lots of physiological and chemical ways it makes you feel good, but there's also the simple enjoyment of actually being out there, training hard or competing in something you've trained hard for, and although it'll hurt, it's a *good* hurt. I'll refer again to Murakami's brilliant quote, 'Pain is inevitable. Suffering is optional.' There have been studies of endurance athletes that show they have a much higher pain threshold than 'normal' people, and that's because ... WE LIKE IT! If you're smashing your hardest out of a race, it's going to hurt, and you suck it up and go faster and harder so that it'll hurt some more. And finishing tired and worn out is the best and safest natural high there is.

Being able to do more—it's great being able to do more with your life. Not just achievement-wise, but from day to day. It feels good to climb mountains with my kids, go on long walks, pop out for a fifty mile bike ride if I've got a spare three hours. I'd much rather that than be able to see another three hours of TV. I'm not sure that anyone when they get older will think to themselves, *I wish I'd watched more TV*. I want to be able to run around with my grandkids (if I have any, no pressure kids!), take them on hikes up Snowdon, take them on long bike rides. And if you train hard for tough races, it's a great feeling when there are no natural limits to your 'normal' days. It's good to feel good about yourself.

Satisfaction finishing a race—I've talked about this before, but it's such a wonderful feeling finishing a race you've worked and trained hard for. Sure, within minutes of finishing you'll inevitably have one of those 'I wonder if I couldn't shaved fifteen minutes off the bike leg' moments, but they're only natural, and a part of progression and growth. But I just love the hours and days after an event, knowing that I've raced hard and to the best of my abilities.

And of course, the refuelling is important too. Don't let anyone tell you that a glass of Yellowtail Shiraz isn't a recovery drink.

Looking better––I'm far from ripped, but I'm OK wearing snug tee shirts. Feeling good about yourself can only give you a more positive mental attitude. Maybe we're edging into that ego place again, but bollocks to it, if you work hard are happy with the way you look, you deserve to feel good about it. I know I could lose a few pounds around the belly, but I also know why I carry those few pounds. Cake. I have much more self-confidence now than I did a decade ago. Maybe it sounds shallow, but most people are the same, and the old adage is true––if you look better, you feel better.

Helping other people––I'm honestly not sure whether what I do has encouraged other people to start exercising as well, but both of my kids are definitely very fitness conscious. My son plays rugby and uses the gym, my daughter runs and goes to the gym, and they're both very fit and healthy and absolutely love the outdoors. I hope a bit of what I've done has influenced them, and I've loved seeing them race in Ironkids races! I always enjoy talking to people about what I do, and when I often get a reaction of disbelief, I'll always tell people, **If I can do an Ironman, virtually anyone can**. I absolutely believe that. It's all about determination, wanting to get there, and being willing to embrace the lifestyle. I remember before my first Ironman I'd watch videos, read accounts, and I was pretty obsessed with the whole thing. Back then I was still juggling doubts about whether I'd even be able to finish, or whether I'd end up a gibbering mess somewhere on mile 80 of the bike or mile 15 of the run. But then I'd see a guy with no legs racing an Ironman ... see the eighty-year-old Iron Nun completing her umpteenth race ... and people in my own club inspired me, too. Being nervous is natural, being positive is essential. And I still believe that virtually anyone can do what I've done, to some extent. You've just got to want it enough.

Sometimes, though, it's good to get help, and maybe here's a good time to talk a little about coaching. I know plenty of coaches through the tri club and beyond, and I know plenty of athletes who pay for coaching. It's purely a subjective thing, and I did spend one year being coached by a great guy from our club, James. He's a superb athlete, a sub-9 hour Ironman, Kona finisher, and I loved the year I had being coached by him. I wanted to really see what I could do for that year, but perhaps my priorities were a bit mixed—I wanted to race two middle distance races to see just how fast I could go, and at the end of the year it was the Brutal (and you can read my race reports about this beautiful, *brutal* race later).

I loved being coached, but I don't think I made the most of it. My problem was not being able to hit all the sessions, and some weeks I barely hit half of them. A lot of this was just being busy with work and family life, but I also know that there's a level of commitment you have to achieve to push yourself really, really hard. I could have got up at 6am on a Saturday to do those 4 or 5 hour rides, but I didn't. So while I've never regretted spending a year being coached by James—he was brilliant, and taught me a lot which I still use now—I don't think I made the most of it.

To be coached properly can be expensive. You can sign up for online coaching, and that's fine for some, but I'm not sure you get much more than you'd get by following pre-designed training plans you can pluck out of books (Don Fink's *Be Ironfit* is brilliant) or online. I think the power and value of a coach is the personal touch—James knew me already, understood that I was likely never going to trouble a podium, and we started our coaching relationship with a good chat about my aims and ambitions. It was a personal touch from beginning to end, and he was always really responsive via text or meeting up at training sessions if I had any questions.

Choosing whether to take on a coach is a very personal decision. I'd recommend it, but bear in mind the the relationship and commitment definitely goes both ways.

16

RACE REPORT:

BRUTAL TRIATHLON, SEPTEMBER 15TH 2018

U p until 2018 the Ironman races I'd done (IM Wales, IM UK, Outlaw) had been big events with lots of supporters and razzamatazz. I'd done a few more gnarly half Ironmans, including the Brutal Half, and that quickly became one of my favourite races. Being someone who's not particularly fast—as I've said before I think I'm distinctly average at all three disciplines, and if I finish in the top half of a racing field I'm happy—I love the tougher, hillier races. There's also something about these smaller events that really appeals to me. No supporters cheering you on all the way around. No music blasting. No residents camped outside their houses getting steadily more pissed lap by lap and shouting as you bike or run by. In an event like the Brutal it's just you against the race, and sometimes there are long, lonely stretches where you don't see another competitor for quite some time. I've tried to analyse why I like this, and I think it's because it's more of a challenge. Cycling though Snowdonia with no one shouting you on really opens you up, exposes any weaknesses or doubts. It's raw. It's brutal. It's *Brutal*. I heard something on the radio this morning that I think applies to races like this. It was a quote from an ultra-runner, who said: "It's ninety percent mental. And the other ten percent is in your head." Wonderful.

This remains one of my favourite races. And that's not the only reason I'll be returning to the Full Brutal in 2021. Read this account from my 2018 race to find out why...

The Brutal

They call it The Brutal. That really should have given me a clue. In truth I knew some of what to expect, because I raced the half distance in 2017 and loved it so much––despite feeling like (and probably resembling) Yoda's little toe by the time I'd finished––that I entered the full distance this year. The organisation, the stunning setting and scenery, the low-key atmosphere, the camaraderie, and the sense of achievement after completing the half convinced me that this should be my big race of the year. And big it was.

So, so big, so long, so epic, it's a day I'll never forget.

So, where to begin? How about the hotel the night before, the fight, the police, the raucous wedding, drunken 2am singing (not by me), the drive-by shootings* (*one of these did not happen). Never one to turn down a weekend away, my lovely wife Tracey came up to support, so I thought we'd treat ourselves and stay in the Royal Victoria Hotel, only about 200 metres from race base. It looked nice from the outside. So did Fawlty Towers. To be fair it wasn't bad on the inside, possessing a sort of it-was-grand-here-30-years-ago charm that I much prefer to the sterile this-could-also-be-a-lunatic-asylum aura of a Premier Inn. It had character. So we checked in and decided to eat straight away. It would be a stretch to call the allegedly thrice-cooked chips once-cooked, but the pizza I had was almost definitely a pizza. The hotel staff were lovely and accommodating (ha ha, oh I kill me, I really do), and it's quirkiness was part of its charm. (And it also meant we got money off our bill. See later.)

After food it was off to do the usual pre-race stuff—register, eye the racing-snake competition and get scared and convinced I haven't done enough training, rack my bike, go to the briefing, dump my stuff in transition so that I can claim a chair for myself, stand staring at my three massive kit-bags and mountain pack slowly convincing myself that I've forgotten just about everything.

All went well, and I was feeling pretty relaxed and eager to get going.

We then went back to the hotel to chill with a very small glass of wine (for me) and an impressively larger glass for Tracey and a bit of mindless Friday evening TV. Except this is when we discovered that the TV didn't work. Oh well. It's wasn't as if I needed my mind distracted from the trials of the following day, or anything.

Entertainment had already settled in another form, however, when a fellow guest had an argument on the second floor and punched his hand through the window, almost showering us with glass as we walked back. We locked ourselves in our TV-less room and piled the furniture against the door (not really, but the thought was there), and watched two police cars and a van turn up.

It had been a long, long evening. It was almost 8pm.

And anyway, who needs sleep the night before what was once voted by Triathlon 220 magazine as 'the world's toughest Ironman'? Eh? What am I, a wimp?

Luckily, the wedding guests drank past feisty, into fighting, and then into a coma by about 1am, their last shred of energy expended in a slurred rendition of a song I'm not sure even they recognised directly beneath our window. And ... I had one of my best night's sleep before an Ironman, ever! I must have had 5 hours! I sprang out of bed at 5am* (*crawled), ate breakfast, went through the usual pre-race nerves and chafe cream application (I did it myself ... this wasn't the time to get distracted), then it was down for the swim.

Water temperature was announced as 16 degrees. Applying the Brutal Quotient, I'd guess maybe 14, but after a bit of ice-cream head I set off and settled into a comfortable rhythm. Lake Padarn is a stunning place to swim. The water is clear and crisp, and whenever you turn for a breath you see staggeringly beautiful scenery. Two laps and out over the timing mat for another two laps, and I was taking longer than I should. It's entirely likely that my 1:26 swim and 4200m recorded on my Garmin was due to my unique swimming technique* (*shit sighting and zig-zagging like someone dodging a sniper's bullet), or perhaps it was that Brutal Quotient again. What, was I expecting this to be easy?

A power walk 200m back to transition with Tracey––up at 5am to support me, bless her!––and then I did something I've never done on an Ironman, or any race, before.

Any guesses?

A full change.

About now is when I should apologise to everyone else in the transition tent. Although a) most other people were stripping off and showing various degrees of naked flesh, and b) after that cold swim no one would have noticed much. T1 must have been 10 or 12 minutes, but every one of them needed. I hadn't really been focussed too much on time, and this was all about comfort. The ride to come was XXXXXXX* long and would be XXXXXXX* tough.

(*fucking)

A quick kiss from Tracey, then I was out onto the bike. Now, a comment here about the weather: right then it was OK. Overcast, a little drizzly, but temperature-wise it was perfect, and I was very comfortable in bib short, a skin, jersey and arm warmers. But more about the weather later. Oh yes.

Five miles into the first bike lap, just after the steepest hill on the route (although far, far, far, far from the longest) I saw a guy by the roadside who appeared to be in trouble. Still standing and holding his bike, he was wobbling and pretty much out of it.

"You okay mate?"

"No, I'm not...."

And when his eyes started rolling and he hit the deck, I knew this was bad. I called the race medic immediately (had the number programmed into my phone. Top tip: ALWAYS DO THIS). In my race-head state and still a bit wobbly myself from the swim, the mileage I gave them was 14 (my average pace to then) instead of mile 5, but luckily they called back 2 minutes later to confirm and I corrected myself. What a numpty.

Meanwhile the guy was sitting against a wall and he'd come around a bit—still dizzy, and with pains in his neck that were worrying me a lot. So we chatted for a while, talked about races we'd done and wanted to do, all the usual triathlete talk, until the medic rocked up. Phew! After chatting to the medic about what I'd seen I shook the guy's hand, wished him luck, and went on my way. I checked in later, and he was OK, but obviously they'd pulled him from the race. Sad, but better safe than sorry.

This half hour stop knocked me for a bit, and it took me a good while to settle back into my bike. The beautiful scenery helped. I really can't think of a more gorgeous place to race––the mountains, the vast skies, the deep, stunning scenery, streams tinkling by the roadside ... just wonderful. It took my mind off the pain. For now.

So, the bike was four epic laps, each about 29 miles. The big part of each lap, and the most stunning, was the climb out of Beddgelert and then up and over Pen-Y-Pas, with a nice descent back into Llanberis. Each lap was around 2,500 feet or so of climbing, and the Pen-Y-Pas climb was a long slow drag, but none of it was too steep.

The first lap felt great, and I'd have done it in about 1:50 without the stop. A quick bottle fill-up, then I was out onto lap 2. I saw a guy a few miles in being helped into the medic's car with blood all over his face, but that was the only accident or mechanical I saw. Considering the weather later in the day, that was a miracle.

Within a few miles my main concern was that I needed a wee. I was trying to take on two-thirds of a litre of water per hour to keep up with my prolific sweat rate (sorry about the detail, but hey ho). Now, around where I live close to Abergavenny there are always field gateways and little nooks and crannies where you can stop, but North Wales seems to be Solid Stone Wall country! I swept down into Beddgelert––a lovely descent into a beautiful town with people sitting outside coffee shops having a lovely cappuccino and cake–– and a few miles later I found what will, henceforth, be known as Tim's Quarry. Three stops on three laps, three pees, one startled goat.

At the end of lap two I saw Tracey, had a hug, and she helped me with nutrition––more gels, more flapjacks, two more bottles of water, and a bag of mini cheddars which went down a treat. Then it was on to Lap 3.

This was getting tougher.

But looming out of the distance, like a giant hauling itself from the rocky terrain of Wales, snarling and drooling and with me, and only me, in its sights, was Lap 4.

And this was when the wind picked up. I'm not sure what speed, but by the time I'd hauled my sorry ass to the top of Pen-Y-Pas and started on that lovely descent back to the end of the bike ride, I was almost having to pedal to move downhill. Two things struck me at this point (besides the heather, litter, and sheep being blown back and forth across the road by the hurricane force winds):

1. If I'd brought my Canyon, I'd have been blown off (not in a good way) and ended up in a wall or a hedge or halfway down a rocky slope.
2. I do this for fun.

It was a tough lap, lap 4. It made me question things. Myself. People who invented bikes and Ironman races. The Brutal Quotient, which means that this bike ride is 116 miles, not 112. But hey, no one said it was going to be easy. I was very happy to get off the bike and hit the changing tent. May I hereby issue apology #2 for any of those who caught an eyeful when I changed, but really by now I was past caring, and I'd just spent almost 9 hours on a bike so GIVE ME A BREAK!

Also on lap 4 I feared I was starting to hallucinate. When one boy racer whizzed past me in a souped up red Renault Clio, so close that I felt the breeze against my legs when he roared by with a splutter of oversized exhaust and fat tyres, I thought it was odd enough. Then two more came. Two more. Two more. I shook my head, blinked a few times.

Two more.

Is this a North Wales thing? That all boy racers are legally obliged to buy a red Renault Clio? A rule probably stipulated by the local Red Renault Clio dealership. Very odd. Very funny. Apart from the tosser who almost hit me.

It was time for the run. Three rocky gnarly laps of the lake, and then up and down Snowdon to finish off. By this time Tracey had gone on her own brutal adventure to climb the mountain on her own and visit the cafe at the top, and I planned on seeing her while I was on the way up and she was coming down. I sort of hoped she might have bought a pasty for me*.

(* she had, but I didn't have it til later. More on that soon).

The wind was really up now, and the mountain tops were no longer in view. On Lap 1 I hooked up with Simon and James, a lovely couple of guys who were probably running a little too fast for me, but they dragged me around that lap and we had a good chat. Unfortunately, they were also bearers of bad news—the whole mountain had been closed due to a severe Red Weather warning, and we'd have to finish our marathon with 2 extra laps of the lake.

My first thought: bollocks. Snowdon is what makes the Brutal *brutal*. It's iconic, and although I was tired and aching and hurting in places I wasn't sure I'd ever been aware of before, I'd been looking forward to that mountain run. But I needn't have worried ... the brutality of those lake laps were destined to come back and bite me.

My first concern after Lap 1 was to check that Tracey was OK. I called from the transition tent and she was on the way back down, having been evacuated from the cafe at the top and told to get back down ASAP just a minute after buying a big cup of tea and a pasty. Yes, she got me one too! But knowing she was OK meant I was OK to head off on four more 5 mile laps of the lake.

Simon and James were a bit too speedy for me so I told them to go on ahead ... and thus began a very lonely few hours. It soon became dark, and by Lap 3 I had to use my head torch full-time. There were a few pockets of support—I'd call them pouches instead of pockets, though they were very vocal and fun—but other than that it was me against the elements.

And the elements were bringing down everything they had. Wind roared and howled along the lake. Pitch darkness fell. A couple of times I found myself walking up slopes with my eyes closed. The feed station on the far side of the lake was an oasis of human contact, light, and glorious jelly babies and mini cheddars, but I was starting to find it really hard going. At one point, mounting a rise, the wind nearly blew me over, and it took my breath away.

There was about 2 solid miles on the far side of the lake which was tough and technical trail running, terrain lit only by the limited splash of my head torch. It was slippery in places, and for tired legs this was very hard going.

4th lap was the worst. I was in a dark place, and also in a dark place. Exhausted, more tired than I'd ever been in a race, I ran 100 seconds and walked for 30. Then walked uphill, and staggered down the trails, careful not to trip and fall.

It really was brutal.

And then the final lap, and the finish line. There was a marshal with my medal, and Tracey, and that was it. Even the finishing arch had been taken down because of the gusting 60mph winds. It was the most subdued finish I've ever seen, but also the most welcome. I had a hug from Tracey—I might have sobbed a little—and the marshal, and then wobbled into the tent for a cup of soup, tea, and a sit down.

Bloody hell. I'd done it. 16:58 hours of racing in the most beautiful, rugged, brutal landscape nature has to offer. I'd never really had a time in mind, but I'm happy with 17 hours (a 'normal; Ironman cut-off time is 17 hours, but for the Brutal it's 21 hours). For most of the run I'd been thinking that I was probably at the tail end of the field, but 48th out of 81 finishers is fine with me, especially with my half-hour stop to help the guy on the bike (without that stop I'd have been 39th).

Physically and psychologically, this was the hardest race I'd ever done, and there were times—long moments—when I really wasn't enjoying it and wondered just what the hell I was doing. But as usual you forget the pain, and the satisfaction and sense of accomplishment kick in.

On reflection, I'm not too disappointed the mountain section of the race was closed (but I am going back in 2021 ... unfinished business!). It doesn't detract from how tough this race is. The extra two laps ensured it was iron distance, and that last ten miles for me was the hardest couple of hours I've ever spent doing anything, ever.

Brutal by name...

PART III

ANOTHER DECADE

"You ran to eat and to avoid being eaten; you ran to find a mate and impress her, and with her you ran off to start a new life together. You had to love running, or you wouldn't live to love anything else...We were born to run; we were born because we run." –– **Christopher McDougall**

17

THEN AND NOW

The Tim of ten years ago wouldn't recognise the Tim of now. As I write this it's December 2020, the end of a long, shitty year (Covid etc), and I'm definitely not as fit now as I have been at various points over the past ten years. But I still exercise 6 days out of 7, and I have an exciting calendar of events already for next year. I'll be adding more soon, for sure. And though I'm in the normal Christmas slump––exacerbated this year because there's been no racing in 2020, even though I've kept up a reasonable level of training––I still know I could probably just about do a half Ironman tomorrow. It would be slow, and it wouldn't be pretty, but I could get there. Continuous endurance training over a period of years puts you in a good place. It's just like riding a bike.

I often tell people that doing an Ironman changed my life, and in many ways that's true. The sense of achievement, the knowledge that you've done something so unbelievably tough, the satisfaction, the can-do attitude you develop by exceeding your own expectations, and sometimes everyone else's too, are all powerful and you can carry them with you forever. Along with the humble-bragging rights.

But really the moment my life changed was the day I met my mate Pete, who'd got fit, and we committed to taking on the National Three Peaks challenge. I still remember going home that evening and telling my wife, and I was buzzing with excitement, anticipation, and a reasonable dose of outright terror. But even then I think something had changed in me. I'd found the thing. The challenge I needed to drive me to get fit. Popping to the gym a couple of times per week, jogging around the lanes now and then, dieting, none of that served a purpose because there *was* no purpose, other than trying to lose weight and get fit. For me, doing that for its own sake never really worked. Having a target in mind is what gave me focus and drive, and I've continued to hone in on tough targets year after year ever since.

Being fit as a by-product of doing something you enjoy so much is the best kind of fitness, the best way to get there, and the best way to *stay* there.

It's become a way of life. An obsession? I wouldn't go quite that far ... although if I go two or three days without exercising I get low and snappy and start climbing the walls. I need my fix! For the first year or two I think people around me viewed it as a bit of a fad, and I do know people who've signed up for their first big event, train for it, do it, then quit. But more people tend to keep going, because there's something addictive about exercise, the way it makes you feel, and the pleasure of doing it. I'm still writing books for a living, which involves me sitting on my arse for several hours each day. The idea of sitting down all evening, too, is just horrible!

When someone new joins our club and says they're only ever doing one Ironman I smile, and nod, and then tell them they'll get the bug. Most of them do. I did, and next year I'll be racing my sixth. I've no plans to stop.

Indeed, as my kids get older, and it's easier to train and travel to race, I can see me racing further afield. Which leads me on to 2019. I was turning 50 that year, and when I saw that my birthday was on a Sunday I thought, *There'll be an Ironman somewhere in the world on that day.* So I did a casual search online.

A day or two later...

Me: 'What do you think about going to Canada for my 50th birthday?'

Mrs L: 'Sounds nice.'

Me: (... smiling ...)

Loaded pause...

Mrs L: 'Is there an Ironman there?'

Me: 'There ... might be.'*

(*There was.)

Fifty years old. Fitter than I was when I turned forty. And thirty. And probably twenty. I'm not kidding myself, I haven't done anything amazing. You read about former drug addicts who now break records racing deca-ironmen, or people who've been diagnosed with terrible diseases who run ultra-marathons. I find anything like this so inspiring now, and I regularly fill up when I'm watching live streams from a finishing line, because I know how emotional crossing that line can be. I understand what each and every one of those finishers has put into their training and racing. I now have an appreciation of effort, and that's something I didn't have ten years ago. Then, watching those weird lycra-clad people sweating and grimacing and running through our local park during the Blaenafon Triathlon, I just thought, *They must be mad. I could never do that.*

Now, I know what it's like.

And believe me, if I can do it, you can too.

18

RACE REPORT:

IRONMAN CANADA—JULY 28TH, 2019

I t was the end of my fifth decade.

And pretty much everyone I've told about this has said, *What an insane way to spend your 50th birthday!* Some of them might have meant that in a negative way, but I sort of agreed with them.

I was spending my 50th birthday racing Ironman Canada in Whistler.

It's a day I'll never forget.

Ironman Canada

And so we landed in Vancouver and drove to Whistler and I competed in Ironman Canada on my 50th birthday and we (me, my wife, our two kids who were then sixteen and twenty) had the absolute holiday of a lifetime. That's the short version. The long version, as anyone who's read my race reports before knows, is ... longer. So settle down with a cuppa. There are bears, spiders, puking runners, potential penalties, bear shit, whales, beers, eagles, and deer (though not all of them were involved in the race).

There's a danger this will become a holiday report rather than a race report, but I'll do my best. Suffice to say, it was very easy to *decide* to do this. The *doing*—from booking everything, to going through some stressful family times beforehand, to actually racing on a different continent—was not so easy. But I wouldn't change a moment of it.

We decided to build a holiday of a lifetime around the occasion. Pointless going all that way for a race, right? So it was Whistler for a week (landing on the Wednesday before Sunday's race), then Vancouver Island to recuperate, then Vancouver for three days before flying home. It was epic.

This was my first race outside of the UK, my fifth Ironman (though the 3rd IM branded race). And from the very beginning I sensed that this was a much more laid back event. The briefing concentrated on the positives, whereas my memory of the IM Wales briefing was a long list of reasons why you could be given a penalty or be DQ'd. In Whistler, the announcer sounded almost apologetic when he mentioned penalties and offences. If you want to hold onto the kayaks for a bit in the swim, you can. If you litter it's a 5 minute penalty (although actually I think this SHOULD be an instant DQ if it's obviously intentional). Very laid back. I liked it!

In fact, the whole organisation was superb. It might have been one of the best organised races I've ever attended. It's a split transition, but it was utterly painless both before and after the race, with shuttle buses taking me and my kit to and from T1, and everything being available in T2 after the race for me and my family to collect. The only slight hiccup was when the crew at special needs on the bike couldn't find my bag. I could have really done with that PB&J bagel and Mars Bar right about then...

So, all the prep done, I hit the sack on the eve of my 50th

birthday nervous, but mostly excited. I knew I could do the distance. I'd witnessed the breathtaking scenery I'd be racing in. And most importantly, I'd decided weeks before that this was going to be a 'fun' race. Training hadn't gone brilliantly (with whole weeks here and there with no training due to work and time away), so for this one I was content to get my money's worth. Besides, why smash myself to pieces for a time, when I'm racing in some of the most beautiful landscape I've ever seen?

So. It was going to be easy.

Right.

Swim...

Meeting at 4:30 in the morning in T1 for the shuttle buses to the swim and T2, getting body marked by volunteers (no tattoo transfers, this was old-style marker pens all the way ... which had totally smeared off by the time I'd sun-creamed up and finished the swim), was a perfect opportunity to mention what day it was.

'Age?' asked the pen-wielding volunteer, ready to write my age group on my calf.

'Fifty. TODAY!'

Cue cheers and whoops and a few 'you must be fucking mad' comments.

Waiting for the swim, daylight dawned, and it was ... beautiful. Just stunning. Water temp was announced at around 19 degrees, and on the distant mountains I could see snow and glaciers. Sun poured across the mountain ranges, a gently glowing palette of oranges and yellows welcoming in the long day to come. I had the first of several emotional moments that would hit me throughout the day, thinking, 'Just look where I'm racing!' A singer sang the Canadian anthem, and there were plenty of tears all around. It was extremely moving, and my usual pre-race nerves were countered by the realisation of how lucky I was, not only to be racing here, but to be racing at all, and to have my family here supporting me all the way. And I looked around at my fellow competitors and saw a similar realisation in many faces. With the sun rising and reflecting from distant glaciers, it was a very Zen moment.

Then I stepped in bear shit.

'Hmm, squishy!' said the guy next to me, squeezing his toes together, and it made a great moment perfect. The cannon fired to commence the rolling start, and I was standing in bear shit at the beginning of Ironman Canada. Some moments you know you'll never forget.

The water was beautiful—clear, perfect temperature—and each time I turned to breathe I saw the wooded, snow covered mountains. I settled into a rhythm and completed the first lap quite comfortably. It was a two lap swim, no exit, and on the second lap I started to suffer. It's been happening for a while on longer swims—numb arms and hands, and this time it got so bad that I just had to use my hands as flippers or oars. Maybe it's bad technique, maybe it's just wear and tear.

Swim completed in 1:26, a pretty bad time when I'd hoped for anywhere between 1:10 and 1:15. Voices of my NEWT club-mates echoed in my head in T1 ('Don't be shit!'). But nuts to it, I was settling in for a long, fun day. And I had the usual 'what do I wear on the bike?' quandary. Plenty of people were heading out just in tri suit, plenty more slipping on a jersey. I wore my bike jersey—pockets for nutrition was part of my reasoning—and perhaps that was a mistake. It was going to get HOT out there.

Bike

The bike course was two long laps. The roads were excellent, the route glorious, and the first lap went pretty well. My strategy had been to aim for an average of 16mph for the whole bike. With 8,500 feet of climbing it's known as one of the toughest on the North American circuit, but ... I didn't find lap 1 that tough. The hills were a pleasant surprise—there were lots of them, but they were all steady and long rather than short and sharp, such as in IM Wales for instance. It was pretty much all up and down with very little flat, but definitely a TT course. I'd elected to hire a road bike, not wanting to face the faff of bringing my Canyon TT thousands of miles deconstructed in a bike box (especially considering my limited mechanical know-how), and I reckon I was one of only 10% of riders not on a TT, or at least a roadie with bars.

No excuses, though. The tough lap 2 was more down to being undertrained than the type of bike I was riding. I still enjoyed it. Sort of. But around mile 90 I had to batter down the creeping voice in my head. 'There's no way you'll finish this. You're knackered. You're undertrained. Do you really think you can run a marathon after this?'

'Sod off,' I replied. 'It's not a marathon, it's an Ironman run.'

I smiled, and looked at the view, and lapped up the areas of support, having received a real boost from seeing my wife and kids on the roadside outside Whistler. They'd made a big banner to wave at me, too! I had to finish this. I had to prove that an old bastard like me could still do an Ironman. So I dug in and—

Oh no. A motorcycle was riding beside me, keeping pace, and I immediately tried to think of what I might have done wrong. I was being ultra careful, but even so everyone here but me rode on the wrong side of the road, and maybe I'd let myself slip once or twice? The ghost of Ironman Wales returned to haunt me...

Then I turned and saw the camera aimed at me.

'I'M FIFTY YEARS OLD TODAY!' I shouted, and that clip made its way into the official IM race recap video.

By mile 100 my right foot was hurting like hell, but I ignored it. It's only pain, right? Pain's temporary, and this was an Ironman! Even so, by the time I handed my bike to a volunteer in T2, the first thing I did was to take off my shoes and breathe a sigh of relief. Maybe wearing the same bike shoes for 5 years isn't the best idea. Maybe I should buy a new pair. Yeah, don't be shit, Tim.

I finished the ride in a moving time of 7:16, but with a couple of stops that averaged out about 15mph. A tough ride, and even though none of the hills had been intimidating, I think the cumulative effect of constant climbing and descending––especially the long 7 mile drag up to the old Olympic Park, averaging maybe 5%––drained me more than I realised.

Run

I saw Tracey and the kids again before the T2 tent, then I headed out onto the run. It was hot now, upwards of 25 degrees or more, and I'd been really careful on the bike to keep myself hydrated. I felt ... surprisingly good. A bit of banter in T2––I told the 6 foot 8 inch guy it wasn't fair and he had to run another 6 miles––then I was out onto the run, and enjoying the more consistent shouts of supports through Whistler. I'd planned to start out and continue at a 10 min mile pace, and for a while this worked. But not for long. I was weakening, and the sun beat down, and I was sweating and sore and now I couldn't get enough fluids into me. I felt queasy at the end of the bike and that continued a little onto the run––something I'd never experienced before––and I saw two runners stop and throw up beside the path. I didn't want to get that bad, so I eased back a little, and started walking through the regular aid stations.

The run was also two laps. A couple of miles around Whistler, then out alongside a couple of beautiful lakes (Lost Lake––no, don't ask me where it was––and Green Lake, almost definitely because it was green), where people were swimming (no thanks, had enough of that for one day) and barbecuing (bastards!), and on Green Lake seaplanes were taking off and landing. The long run out alongside Green Lake was particularly tough, and hitting Whistler at the end of lap 1, with a half marathon to go and hearing people finishing, was torture.

But I was smiling, saw my lovely family, enjoyed the support, the surroundings were beautiful, and I reminded myself again and again how bloody lucky I was to be doing this somewhere so wonderful. Chatting to fellow runners helped ('Hello, did I tell you I'm fifty today?'), and the marshals were uniformly excellent. Aren't they always? But in Canada ... well, they were Canadians, and something we learned on our holiday is that Canadians might just be the nicest people on the planet.

For the second lap I ran for a mile and walked for a 100 seconds, and that tactic seemed to work. And then I ran into Whistler for the finish, hearing the cheering from a mile or two away, trying to run all the way in, and when I hit the long road leading to the finish chute ... the route jigged left and doglegged for another couple of hundred metres. That was the hardest and the best part of the run for me, and even though my time was entirely forgettable, my whole day had been remarkable. It had been painful, and a struggle, and I had to shove down moments of self-doubt ... but wonderful.

Tracey and Dan were waiting at the finishing chute. I almost ran past them, then spotted them and went in for a kiss and fist-bump. Ellie was waiting for me at the finishing arch to take pics, and I ran in with the announcer saying 'Happy birthday Tim Lebbon, you are an Ironman, Tim!' Epic. (But didn't anyone tell him I was 50?)

Something else that was refreshingly different at the finish was the attention given to the athletes. The moment I crossed the line a volunteer zeroed in on me, gave me my medal, a foil blanket, a bottle of water, my tee shirt and cap, and she said 'Lean on me if you need to.' I might have felt a little bit emotional. She insisted that she saw me out of the finishing compound and into the care of my family. I might also have told her that it was my birthday, and she gave me an extra IM Canada Finisher's flag. Nice one!

I met the gang and hobbled across to where they were giving out the pizza. Pepperoni. Pretty standard. But perhaps the best pizza on Planet Earth at that precise moment.

14:30 isn't a great time, but what a remarkable race. And that's what I always intended. Canada is an incredible place, and finishing that race was just the start of a wonderful holiday I had with my lovely family. We went white-water rafting and kayaking and hiking, saw a bear and an eagle and a whale and ospreys and deer and seals, my son got bitten by a spider (no super-powers as yet... unless eating is a super-power), ate some wonderful food and drank some splendid local brews, and made loads of great memories.

I'll always remember where I was and what I did on my 50th birthday.

19

MY SIXTH DECADE

Somehow, I'm fifty-one years old.

It creeps up on you. Time. I don't think I feel fifty-one, whatever the hell that's supposed to feel like. I still love rock music and listen to it all the time. I enjoy finding new bands. I love going to gigs (when I can ... 2020 has been a bit shit on that front. On every front, in fact). I've always been bald (hair never suited me), but recently a friend on Zoom said 'How long has your beard been grey, Tim?' And someone else in a work Zoom meeting, when talking about all the horror I write, said 'But you're such a nice man!' *Man* makes me sound really old! I guess there's no fooling Time, but we can do our best to ward it off. And I'm going to be training and racing for as long as my body lets me, and then probably beyond that, too. There are a few aches and pains now, for sure, but that comes with the territory.

Getting fit in my forties is still one of the very best things I've ever done. Actually, I guess that 'getting fit' subtitle is misleading, because it didn't take me the whole decade to do it. But 'getting fit early in my forties then trying to maintain that fitness for the whole decade, with a few slumps and then a few moment of deeper determination, and too much cake' doesn't sound so snappy.

And I'm not slowing up because I've hit and passed my half century. Far from it. 2020 was a blip, and all my 2020 races have been rolled over to '21. So in 2021 I'm looking forward to the Outlaw Half, Windsor Triathlon, Long Course Weekend, and then in September I'm confronting the mighty Brutal again. My target is to finish in the top third of the field, so a sub-15:30. I'll be signing up for more events, too, with my eye on an ultra-marathon in November (possibly the Lemur Loop which I did a couple of years ago), and a couple of long sportives in the spring.

So, it's going to be fun.

I hope you've enjoyed this meandering, personal, occasionally profane, and often rambling account of my ten years of adventures, pain, racing, training, sweat, chafing, medals and cake. I've certainly enjoyed writing it and visiting those times again, always with the knowledge that I'm doing this for fun! In closing, I'll repeat what I've said several times before, for anyone who might have picked this up for a bit of inspiration, or even a bit of a push in the right direction:

There's no downside to getting fit. And if I can do it, anyone can.

And in 10 years's time, keep your eyes open for *Still Running, Walking, and Crawling—Staying Fit in My Fifties*!

Okay ... it's cold outside, but sunny, and I'm finishing this up just before lunch. It's the perfect time for a run.

"Run when you can, walk if you have to, crawl if you must;
just never give up."
– Dean Karnazes

ACKNOWLEDGMENTS

Once you start thanking people, you'll inevitably leave someone out, and that person 'knows people', and that's how the best revenge thrillers begin, and ... but maybe I've been reading and writing too much horror. So here goes.

Massive thanks to my brilliant triathlon club the NEWTs. Picking individual friends from that splendid organisation is impossible, so this is a catch-all 'thank you' for the help, advice, and inspiration that helped to get this former fat bastard's arse around some of the toughest races in the world. Joining NEWT is one of the best things I've ever done.

Thanks to Pete Lyons for the original three words—'I got fit'—that started a real change in my life. And to Andy Holgate and Andy Baxter who helped that change happen.

Thanks to so many good friends who took an interest (and who perhaps weren't so interested, but still put up with me banging on about races I'd done and experiences I'd had whilst resisting the inclination to tell me to shut up). These friends are too numerous to mention by name, and for that I am very, very grateful. I have always been rich with friends, and that's the greatest wealth there is.

Thanks to all the wonderful people who offered such nice words about this book for cover and promotional purposes ... you're all legends, and I feel very blessed. And to Seán O'Connor and Kealan Patrick Burke for help above and beyond in book design and production (this self-publishing is all new to me).

To my lovely extended family who have always been so encouraging, even whilst offering a sometimes bemused glance.

And finally to my wife Tracey, and kids Ellie and Dan. What can I say? They're put up with so much—me spending hours away training, my sweaty kit discarded around the house, bikes and trainers all over the place, a grumpy git in the house when he's injured, an anxious git as races approach ... and they've been there supporting me for every Ironman race I've done. At the end, when I've stumbled over the line, they always tell me how knackered they are. I love you guys.

ABOUT THE AUTHOR

Tim Lebbon is a New York Times-bestselling writer of more than 45 novels. His stories have been filmed by Hollywood as 'Pay The Ghost' and 'The Silence', he's won a few awards, and he has more books due out soon. He loves triathlon, cake, and real ale, and hair never suited him.

If you enjoyed *Run Walk Crawl*, please check out other books by Tim, although his novels are not generally as light-hearted and contain less lycra.

You can find his books in all the usual bookstores and online, and a great place to begin is his website: www.timlebbon.net

Made in the USA
Coppell, TX
18 March 2021